THE 8 PATHWAYS TO FINANCIAL SUCCESS

2/3/99

To Sue,

Enjoy! Hope you have some fun with this

Warmest regards
Bob

Also by ROBERT BUECHNER

Accumulating Wealth with before-tax Dollars
(with David Manzler)

Why Universal Life
(with David Manzler and Thomas Eason)

Prosper through Tax Planning

Living Gangbusters

The 8 Pathways To Financial Success

ROBERT BUECHNER

ISBN: 0-938067-56-7

Printed in the United States of America.

DEDICATION

To my father who taught me to spend less than I made, to invest in the stock market for the long haul, and to put family first.

CONTENTS

ACKNOWLEDGEMENTS

I am grateful to the many people who have made a significant contribution to this book.

My legal secretary, Cathy Mullis, not only provided hours upon hours of word processing skills but also was a source of frequent, constructive criticism. My law partner, Frank Marnell, performed the difficult task of editing the final product. And my good friend and child psychologist, Christopher Rich, helped significantly in the early going with the structure and organization of the book.

In addition, the following people helped with specific chapters and ideas: Dayle K. Rust, clinical director of a personal growth clinic in Las Vegas, Nevada, with the psychological concepts presented throughout; Thomas Johnson, with the income tax chapters; Dale Wilson with the oil and gas information; and James E. Simpson, Jr., CLU, with the chapter on insurance.

Thanks also to my firm's law associate, Vasanth R. Shenai, for all of his help in the most recent update of the book.

PREFACE

Some of us live and die by changes in our financial status. The accumulation of wealth is a serious matter, but it presents no greater challenges than many other areas of our lives. Yet it is an area that often receives a disproportionate part of our time, energy, and concern.

Becoming financially successful is a comprehensible, controllable process. It requires persistence, discipline, knowledge, and professional assistance. The process for financial growth is basically the same for each of us although there may be great differences in where we each begin.

My job as a tax attorney has been to help clients accumulate and preserve wealth. Through education, professional referral, and document preparation I have helped clients progress in their financial growth.

Based on my work with clients, I have delivered a multitude of seminar programs concerning the eight pathways to financial success. Condensing, editing, and reshaping these seminar programs has resulting in the creation of this book which is about the process of successful financial planning. In many respects, this book represents the compilation and summarization of over $1,000,000 of tax, financial and legal advice.

The beauty of the financial growth process presented herein is that it works. It has worked for my clients. It has worked for me and it will work for you. By reading this book, going through the analyses presented and taking the steps indicated, you will increase your financial prosperity. Of course, the choices you make will have a dramatic impact on how successful you are. But by taking the first step and reading this book, you'll guarantee financial progress, growth, and success and probably eliminate a few mistakes already made by others who have traveled this pathway before you. "The wise man borrows from the mistakes of others, the fool insists on paying for his own experience."

Introduction

If you are like me and most other Americans, you find the subject of personal financial planning both very interesting and very unpleasant. Much of the unpleasantness stems from the inadequacy of almost everyone's finances. Even if our present incomes are sufficient to meet our current financial needs (true for fewer than half of all Americans), we worry about how we can possibly finance our childrens' educations, or whether the Social Security System will survive to our retirement. According to the United States Department of Commerce, only about 5 percent of all Americans currently achieve financial independence by age sixty-five. Even those who do reach that goal often spend inordinate amounts of time worrying about whether or not their nest egg is being adequately protected.

A second unpleasant aspect of financial planning is the unpredictability and increasing instability of the national and international financial environment. In recent years we have had to contend with an energy crises, runaway inflation, high interest rates, capriciously changing tax laws, massive federal deficits, national and international scandals in the financial markets, and a highly uncertain global economic future. In this kind of environment, the task of planning for our own financial needs over a period of a decade or even years seems nearly impossible. In addition, we sometimes are dismayed by the complexity of the investment opportunities available to us. In an era of virtually instantaneous electronic funds transfer, we can move our liquid assets back and forth among common stocks, corporate bonds, real estate, government debt instruments, mutual funds, preferred stocks, and money market instruments. We can invest in insurance plans of increasing complexity and sophistication, limited partnerships of different types, real estate deals, new venture start-ups, fine arts and collectibles, commodities and precious metals, and many other forms of investment. When faced with this bewildering array of choices and decisions, many of us are tempted to throw up our arms in despair and simply avoid the whole confusing and depressing topic of personal financial planning.

Finally, it is a difficult matter to find satisfactory professional help to advise us concerning financial planning. The problem is not that there is not a sufficient array of professionals to assist us in our attempts to master our own financial situation. There are multitudes of experts we can call on, including stockbrokers, insurance agents, business brokers, real estate brokers, certified financial planners, bankers, accountants, lawyers, investment counselors, and financial planners, all of whom may have excellent financial advice for us. However, it is very difficult to know what expert we need at what time. Moreover, many of the experts have expertise in only one or a few areas, and they may have a vested interest (their own income) in persuading us to follow their advice in only one limited area.

In a nutshell, the problem is that we lack a clear understanding of the total financial picture; our goals and individual resources are so different, and the range of choices open to us is so broad, that there are no simple, comprehensive rules that all of us can follow all of the time.

The intent of this book is specifically to organize the overwhelming complexity of personal financial planning. What Mr. Buechner presents in the following pages is a conceptual model of the total planning process which will enable you to make sense of the complexity. He calls his model the "Eight Pathways" model, and through becoming familiar with it, you will become better able to evaluate your total financial planning program. This book is not intended as a do it yourself guide which will enable you to do without the advice of a tax attorney, certified public accountant, an investment counselor, an insurance agent, or whatever other professional experts you may have used or considered using. Rather, it will enable you more confidently to develop and evaluate your own comprehensive financial plan, to clarify your goals, and to identify what's reasonable to expect from whatever kinds of investments or types of professionals you become involved with. The result just might be that you will sleep a little better at night, more comfortable that your financial planning efforts will produce the kinds of results that we are all looking for.

Personally, I have already found the "Eight Pathways" model to be extremely useful and I strongly recommend the following pages to you.

Andrew C. Eustis, Ph.D.
Xavier University
Director, Center for
Management and Professional
Development

AUTHOR'S NOTE

My purpose in writing this book is to give you concise, understandable information that will help you make your life more successful. But why should you choose my work product as your guide to success over any other text?

As a professional, my background makes me as qualified as anyone to write on tax, insurance and financial matters. Moreover, I differ from other professionals who specialize in the tax and financial areas is that I have been a student of psychological principals for over 20 years. I have been through extensive training and have learned from my clients as well as from my own experiences what it takes to achieve the highest levels of success. I have also been made aware of some of the more common pitfalls we all have to avoid in our life's journey.

In a nutshell, I can tell you that attitude is every bit as important as technical knowledge in achieving financial success. I credit the success I have been able to achieve as an attorney to knowledge, follow through and a genuine love for my clients. I have found that clients remain clients only as long as that caring attitude is present. More important, I choose to be a caring professional for what it brings me intrinsically.

Becoming a financial success is a little more difficult than simply becoming successful in one's chosen field. Values need to be prioritized, goals need to be set, short-term desires sometimes need to be stifled for long term gains. Moreover, a basic understanding of various technical rules must be mastered which is why there are eight pathways to financial success.

Simply reading this book will not make a significant difference in your life. You need to work through the exercises presented, reexamine your goals and objectives and follow through with the proper planning. Then this book can make a vast difference in the success you achieve. You have my word on it!

Bob Buechner

CHAPTER 1
AN OVERVIEW

Financial success is not about turning our lives into a balance sheet or income statement. Financial success is about achieving and maintaining peace of mind about our financial affairs as we journey through life.

People from all walks of life have the opportunity to be financially successful. They key is that they can achieve peace of mind through proper financial planning and goal setting.

This book deals with the concept of both living in balance as well as keeping financial planning and investments in balance. There is no substitute for balance in our lives and its importance cannot be overstated.

Balance

Does it make any sense to you to think of having your net worth double at the expense of your family relationships? Or, how about having your health deteriorate because you are concerned about some investments that you have made? Yet, these are common factors that people face that evidence a lack of control over their lives when it comes to dealing with financial matters. Financial issues need to be limited to what they are and limited to the fact that they are just one aspect of our life. We do not want financial problems or opportunities to spill over and impact on the joy of living. Consequently, it is very important that financial goals be set in a way that are consistent with how much time and effort we are able and willing to spend and not cause our entire life to center around what we are doing financially. The purpose of our lives is to become better human beings, not to turn ourselves into gold coins.

The concept of balance is presented in more detail in the final chapters of this book. However, it is important to mention at the beginning that we not only need to have plans for what we are doing financially and set goals in these areas but we should be doing the same in other areas of our lives. Goal setting is what helps us set our course and activate our minds to achieve the success that we seek.

Before getting into a detailed discussion of various concepts, an overview is presented of the entire book. This provides you with a road map as to where you are headed on your journey through this book.

Tax Legislation

We can't stop planning or writing books simply because there is more tax legislation on the horizon. But we can be mindful of huge federal deficits and the perceived need to raise taxes.

With regard to future tax legislation, it is this author's belief that (1) tax rates will decrease for the middle and lower income individuals but not for higher income tax payers, (2) some estate planning options will be eliminated, and (3) the Roth IRA will not last forever.

The Heart of Successful Planning

We first consider the general principles of any successful planning, not just financial planning. Having some information on successful planning can help with understanding and applying the other more technical information in the book.

The heart of any successful planning consists of the process of orienting our thinking and behavior towards setting and achieving goals. Recent studies of millionaires have revealed that an individual's attitude has much more to do with his level of success than any other characteristic such as education, family, or social-economic background. The language of success is introduced to help keep us on the right track and to help us develop the attitude which will be most productive for goal achievement. We can establish goals by examining our personal values and developing a conscious sense based on those values of what we choose to achieve in our lives. Prioritization of our values is essential to the prioritization of our goals. Once we have goals we learn to apply the so called law of optional behavior which is akin to the principal of deferred gratification to help us achieve our goals.

The Eight Pathways

The eight pathways are eight separate areas of concern in financial planning. Although one pathway or another may loom larger at a given time than the others, all eight must be kept in mind fairly consistently over your life in order to bring about full financial success. Each pathway is given a separate chapter in this book.

The first pathway is that of cash flow management. This pathway covers a broad area of concern because it deals with both the generation of cash through one's vocation and the process of budgeting for the disbursement of that income. It is vitally important that an individual be concerned about his profession and business because this is the golden goose for accumulation for wealth. Furthermore, the proper attitude has to be developed with regard to budgeting; discipline must be maintained and short term pleasures must be sacrificed to long term objectives.

If you were planning to drive across the country, you would certainly bring with you sufficient cash, credit cards or checks to enable you to continue your journey in case your car broke down. The second pathway is insurance because we need to provide for protection and backup in the event that something happens to impede our long-term plan to work, prosper, save money, and accumulate wealth. The purchase of adequate insurance for health, disability, and life protection enables the individual to earn the right of passage to other investments and planning ideas. Without adequate insurance, the best financial plan in the world can reach a dead end upon the occurrence of a tragedy. You might say that the purchase of adequate insurance of all types is your ticket to the game of investing. Unless you have a ticket you are subject to being thrown out at any time.

Pathways number three, four and five have to do with investments. The three types of investments to be distinguished are low-risk, low return; moderate risk, moderate return; and high risk, high return. The degree to which an individual should be involved in any of these investments is a personal matter. Some professionals recommend that an investor maintain sufficient liquidity in safe, accessible vehicles to cover living expenses for a three month period. Individuals who are nearing retirement should not have much money in high-risk, high return investments. Younger people who have available excellent high-risk investment opportunities, may want to have up to one-third of their money in high-risk, high return investments, while a person at retirement age should only have perhaps a tenth of their net worth in high risk, high return investments. The most important overall concept in the investment area is diversification. Individuals should invest only in areas where they have an understanding and can accept the fluctuations in the value of their investment as market conditions and economics change. An individual should have an array of investments that will do well in the long run whether or not we have a return to high inflation and high interest. This means having a balance between long term investments and short term investments that will allow flexible reaction to changes in interest rates. Experience has proven that one may violate these percentages and may outperform the averages for a short period of time, (5 to 7 years) but if you place your entire net worth in a high-risk, high return mode for a long enough period of time you are destined for a financial roller coaster.

Pathways six, seven and eight have to do with the technical categories of income tax planning, retirement planning and estate planning. In general, the payment of taxes frustrates the accumulation of wealth. To the extent possible it is desirable to eliminate or defer the payment of taxes as long as possible. The chapter on income tax planning discusses the techniques that are available for deferring income from one year to the next as well as the techniques that are available for accumulating funds for the payment of college expenses. The chapter on retirement planning presents the ways in which our system encourages individuals to save for retirement, sets forth some ideas on how to establish goals for the wealth needed at retirement, and considers how to achieve those goals. One important concept of retirement planning is that it should not be of overwhelming importance - people who emphasize retirement planning to the exclusion of other investments may very well miss important, if not aggressive, opportunities for investment that sometimes occur in a busy life. Finally, the chapter on estate planning emphasizes the importance of having a proper will, and if needed, a trust, and reviews the fundamental ideas for avoiding federal estate taxes.

The Elements of Financial Planning

The eight pathways set forth the financial areas in which we each need to set goals and make plans to achieve them. Yet, there would be a missing ingredient in this presentation if we did not discuss the process for how each of us gets from where we are to the financial status we desire. This process is what is commonly referred to as financial planning.

Financial planning is the process of collecting and analyzing data, setting and prioritizing goals, making and implementing plans to achieve those goals, and monitoring your progress. If you are a disciplined person and fairly sophisticated in financial matters, you can probably function as your own financial planner. If, on the other hand, you believe you need some help in establishing a sense of direction and follow through, you should consider hiring a professional financial planner.

Whether or not you hire a person to help you with the financial planning process, you will need one or more professionals to help you with the implementation of your plans.

The Role of Professionals

As you develop goals for each of the eight pathways, you should also identify the professionals you want to consult to help you achieve those goals. In some areas, such as cash flow management and high risk investments (for example, if you like selecting your own individual securities), you may function as your own adviser. But at least identify who is responsible to help you achieve the goals you have set in each of the eight pathways.

Part of the key to making the most of your professional assistance is understanding the role that each professional can and should play. To help you with this, the chapter on professionals includes a discussion of the role of the financial planner, the accountant, the investment adviser, the account executive, the insurance agent and the attorney. These are the people who can make an important difference in how easily you achieve your financial objectives.

Balance in Financial Planning And In Our Lives

The final concept presented in this book deals with balance - first, in the area of financial planning and then in the area of our lives. It is not productive in the long run for us to do a great job of income tax planning if all the money we save is consumed or invested poorly. Similarly, it does not make much sense for us to have great wealth if the rest of our life is coming apart. Balance is needed so that our goals work together and not against one another.

Prioritization of our financial goals involves the same process as prioritization of other life goals. We need to determine what is most important to us and what steps we must take to achieve what we value. Completion of the prioritization process gives us goals and plans in each of the Eight Pathways. We can apply the same process to keep our financial affairs in balance with the rest of our lives. This is how we become true masters of the financial game.

Asset Protection

Once you have accumulated some assets, it may then become very important to you as to how those assets are held to be free from the claims of creditors.

There are several risks that we always face. One is the risk that investments we make can wipe out some of our savings. The other risk is that something may happen to us, whether it is a professional error or whether it is a car accident, that can create liability for us that far exceeds whatever insurance limits we have. Because of the uncertainties we each face in our lives, Appendix A is included that presents some basic thoughts on asset protection and gives you some ideas for diversification and how assets are held.

Chapter 2
The Heart Of Successful Planning

Becoming financially successful is no more difficult than becoming successful in any other area of our life. It requires some creativity, goal setting, good planning, and, occasionally, a touch of luck. This chapter will discuss the foundation for success for all walks of life.

We begin our look at successful planning by considering the language of success. Language changes are relatively easy ones to make and can lead to changes in both attitude and behavior. Also, using the language of success is part of the next area of discussion, which concerns orienting our mind for success. Experience teaches us that the best results are obtained in whatever we do when we combine positive self-expectation with the proper action. If we are sick, this action may include taking medicine. If we are doing financial planning, this action may include setting up a budget or changing our investment strategy. In order to determine the proper action, we need to utilize our mind in the most productive manner possible. This means being able to understand the conflict that often exists between the thinking and feeling parts of our minds and acting in a way that is most consistent with our goals. As an additional part of our discussion on choosing the proper behavior, we consider the law of optional behavior, which tells us why it can be so helpful to us to control the feeling part of our minds and to defer gratification when we are working toward a goal. Finally, we discuss goal setting, which should take place in order for us to have a clear picture of where we want to head.

The Language of Success

Our internal language may need to be improved to make it more useful. Some language can be immobilizing or can color life's possibilities beyond reasonable expectations. Either way can create a problem for future action. We can develop this language from unrealistic expectations or negative experiences.

The following are true life language descriptions of various investments:

"I've lost my shirt in every limited partnership I've ever purchased."

"They've hit oil big. It's gushing out. I'll be rich!" (This was on a $10,000 investment).

"This was a bad deal, I've lost everything and now IRS wants more."

The person who has lost his shirt in every limited partnership investment may, or may not be, totally accurate. In any event, it is unlikely, with such a jaundiced view, that he will ever invest in another limited partnership, regardless how strong the investment opportunities are that are presented to him. The oil investor, on the other hand, will likely take all his oil profits, and whatever other monies he can find, and invest in more oil properties. Each of these people is probably headed for problems.

The more reasonable way to think about and talk about investment results is by describing them as either *productive* or *non-productive*. These words take the place of good and bad, right or wrong, good and evil, bright and stupid, sinful or sinless. The reason we like to use these words is that they tend to be non-judgmental. A lot of negative words tend to be immobilizers, whereas the word non-productive automatically can cause us to shift to what is productive behavior. If it is productive, fine. Let's put the same formula to use elsewhere (same advisors, etc.). If it is non-productive, fine. Let's see what we've learned and what we can do differently in the future to try to make it productive.

Let's rephrase the "lost my shirt" scenario. "Limited partnerships for me have been largely non-productive. I am either very unlucky or I haven't been working with the right advisors. I need someone who can tell me what is the right type of investment for me if I want to be a passive investor with limited exposure. Also, I now know that I need to get a professional involved to give me a second opinion."

The language of success also requires that we treat our mistakes with some respect. Mistakes are very different from failure and are simply part of the growth process. The person who wants to go through life without any mistakes is like the prizefighter who wants to become world's champion without ever getting hit. People who are afraid of mistakes are probably also afraid of making decisions. This would be a failure. Mistakes are an important part of our growth and there is probably much more for us to learn from our mistakes than from our successes. Try referring to mistakes as learning experiences to change your perspective.

Finally, there does not have to be anything in our lives that we call a problem — there are only challenges and opportunities which, when met, become prelude to reward. Problems tend to frustrate us and to cause us anxieties and render us immobile. Challenges and opportunities, on the other hand, when recognized as such, can bring out our creativity and give us a feeling of excitement about what is ahead of us.

The language of success helps us look at what we can do with what we have in front of us. It gets us out of a reacting mode and into one of creative planning and action. The language of success helps us attain a positive self-expectation and thereby orient our minds to success. It enables us to move more quickly and more easily from the non-productive to the productive.

Orienting Our Minds For Success

Physicians have known for some time that not every drug has the same effect on each of us and may on some of us have no effect at all. Suppose you were told a drug works in 60% of the cases - would you take the drug? If you were a physician, what would you do about the 40% for whom the drug seems to have no effect? Tough question. A number of us do much better in responding to medicine that others - in fact, physicians have found some people respond as well to a placebo (a pill that has no real effect, such as a sugar pill) as others do to regular medicine. Basically, all that a placebo does is give the person a reason to get well. A person who takes a placebo thinking that it will have a beneficial effect orients his mind to expect good things to happen. Positive thinking is important but it is the taking of the pill, not the belief or thinking, that is the most important aspect in this process. In psychological circles, this is called acting upon positive self-expectation. Perhaps the 60% who get well with a given drug either strongly believe it will be effective for them or their bodies just respond to the drug taken. But most often it is both their expection combined with the drug's physical properties which result in the highest degree of success.

Putting positive self-expectation into action is a fundamental and important part of the psychology of success. We need optimistic, successful attitudes in order to design and achieve the kind of success that we desire.

Having and using an optimistic attitude will develop confidence in our ability to achieve success and can pay tremendous dividends. When we take medicine, we orient the mind to look for something to happen within our bodies. Similarly, when we establish goals that we are intent to achieve, we orient the subconscious to be on the lookout for some new productive ideas and opportunities. Financial success comes to the person who has not only taken steps to achieve it, but who has made himself ready for it. Do not be surprised if, in the course of following through with the action plans suggested in this book, you experience a surge of creativity that leads you to some very productive opportunities.

Affective and Cognitive Domains

Information about how the mind works can enable us to develop the correct behavior to more easily achieve our desired goals.

Although psychologists are the first to admit this is a simplification, they tell us that the human mind is essentially split into two parts: the feeling part and the thinking part. The feeling part is called the Affective Domain and the thinking part is called the Cognitive Domain. The Affective Domain is where our feelings, thoughts, and, consequently, all our motivations for behavior originate.

The key to success is learning how and when to use each side of our brain most effectively. It may seem very complex at first, but it becomes easier with experience. First you decide where you want to go, or what you want to achieve, and set a definite goal and objectives to get there (the "how-to's"). Both sides of the brain (the affective and the cognitive) usually work quite well together in the planning stages of setting goals and objectives. Conflict between the Affective and Cognitive Domains will, most often, come only when your plans and goals involve a change that you think would be productive but feelings do not give support to (such as thinking it would be desirable to repair your automobile when on a feeling level you would love a new car). This is the prime time to use the reasoning process of the cognitive mind and act with your reasoning and in variance to your feelings. Studies have shown that when you develop your cognitive brain, you improve your willpower and your success escalates. When you don't, you recycle and eventually find yourself, basically, back where you started. When you have set a well thought out goal, you don't need permission from your feelings to "move your feet." In fact, if it's a change you're after, most often feelings will try to get you to postpone or modify your action. You experience the natural conflict between your Affective and Cognitive Domains.

So you can see, even though we would like support from our feelings in order to change our behavior, such support isn't essential, or important, for us to be effective in reaching our goals. What is essential is that we ACT as if we did have support from our feelings.

This was demonstrated by the noted French physician Dr. Emile Coue years ago. He helped literally thousands of people affect a cure of a wide range of problems. His prescription for them was to repeat aloud five times a day, "Every Day in Every Way, I Am Getting Better and Better and Better." Skeptics who didn't believe, but followed Dr. Coue's prescription anyway, were cured nevertheless. Mental health professionals have an explanation for this phenomenon. They say the loud repetitions are received by the subconscious, which automatically directs the healing powers of the body to begin the healing process. It is the ACTION toward the goal that initiates the process on the intuitive level of the mind which is so powerful when compared to only a conscious intellectual process.

Drs. Jellison and Humphrey in their writing "Forget About Positive Thinking - It's What You Do that Counts," concluded that, in reality, the belief (the positive thinking) is beneficial but what they found was really important to success was "more getting out in the field and doing, even if we do fall flat on our faces a few times."

So let's do it and learn how to do it better.

The *motivation* for our *behavior* originates from the Affective (feeling) Domain. Most often, neither the motivation nor the behavior is screened by the Cognitive (thinking) Domain. In fact, most of our behavior (some psychologists believe as much as 95%) can take place without our conscious awareness. It is best described as a conditioned response or a reflex action. Sometimes we drive a car for miles, even in traffic, without a conscious focus or awareness of what we are doing. Yet we can consciously respond and become instantly aware if anything out of our ordinary experience of driving happens. What originates in the Affective Domain is our habit behavior. When we become aware that our habit behavior is not productive (usually too late), we then want to change to be productive.

Before we act, the Cognitive Domain can screen or review the choice of behavior that is prompted by the Affective Domain. For example: we may feel like yelling at our child - the Cognitive Domain can screen this prompted or motivated behavior and determine if the prompted behavior is consistent with our pre-determined goals. If the prompted behavior is consistent, we yell, if not, we select and use a behavior that is consistent with our goals. The Cognitive Domain performs the reasoning function, but does so effectively only if we have developed goals.

Since we now believe that most of our behavior is a conditioned response below the conscious level, acting on the feelings from the Affective Domain, it is also important to know that this doesn't cause a problem for most of us most of the time. In the average person, approximately 80% of our conditioned response behavior is productive behavior. But this does tell us that there are some things that we do out of habit or conditioned response without going through the reasoning process which may be non-productive. What can we do about the approximate 20% of prompted behavior originating from the Affective Domain that is not helpful for us?

One of the challenges of our lives is to recondition or change our non-productive behavior. This can be done by setting goals and then monitoring our behavior to see if our behavior is consistent with our goals. If it is not, then we can choose to change our behavior. When we measure our prompted behavior against our goals, we are using the cognitive part of our mind. This means we run our choice of behavior through our reasoning tunnel before we initiate action.

We can use the Cognitive Domain for setting goals and then check our behavior against those goals. Here is an example.

An individual decides that he wants to lose 20 pounds. He sets his objectives to accomplish this which includes not eating any candy until his goal has been achieved. He is offered some M&M candies and his emotional conditioned response (Affective Domain) is "yummy." His affectively motivated behavior is to eat them, but as he reaches for them, he first thinks about his objective of losing 20 pounds. He transfers the issue of eating the M&M's from his Affective Domain, which would have him eat the M&M's, to the Cognitive Domain, which means he runs it through the reasoning tunnel to determine if the behavior is consistent with his goals. He asks himself the "golden question" before selecting an action. "Is this action consistent with my goals?" In this case the answer is no. Once the reasoning process is complete, he then refrains from eating the M&M's unless he rationalizes (also known as "rational lies") that maybe he can eat the M&M's and skip dinner or eat only the chocolate-coated peanut M&M's. Without having, and examining, the goal of losing 20 pounds, he would not have had any cause to have shifted the issue of eating M&M's into his Cognitive Domain where it was governed by a pre-established goal or objective.

This same approach is valid in financial planning or in any other aspect of our life. The process of goal setting is fundamental to establishing behavior that will lead to actualization of the proper goal. Suppose an individual has made the decision that he is going to invest some of his extra cash in a real estate investment that will have a chance to appreciate substantially and will also spin off some tax benefits. While he is looking for a proper investment, he is approached by a friend who has a $25,000.00 boat for sale. He has always wanted a boat and feels that this is an excellent buy. His prompted response is "buy," but when he looks at this purchase in line with his goal to invest, he declines the purchase and saves his money for the real estate investment.

The Law of Optional Behavior

William Glasser in his book *Positive Addiction* provides us with a very instructive law governing behavior which applies to our lives in general, including planning for financial success. In striving to achieve our goals, the law of optional behavior is a law, like the law of gravity, that governs the effect of our choice of behavior or action. When we have established goals and are working towards those goals, we will be faced with choices in behavior. When we have a choice as to what action we do, certain feelings will follow that action. The law of optional behavior is that these feelings will either (1) be good now but bad later or (2) bad now but good later. Thus, the behavior we choose can have a dramatic impact on how we feel in the present as well as how we feel in the long-term.

If you have the opportunity to do something and to feel good about it now but bad about it later versus feeling bad about it now but good about it later, what do you do? Most successful people who are asked this question choose that behavior which causes them to feel bad now but good later. Like the person who wanted to lose 20 pounds, eating the M&M's at the time would have been a pleasurable experience for him that he would have regretted and felt badly about later. While not eating the M&M's at that time was not pleasant but consistent with his goals, he feels good about it later. That is normal for the bad feeling comes from fear, a sense of denial, or uncertainty. Experience and reason has taught us that the bad feelings, when experienced first, last a measurable amount of time, whereas the good feelings last an indefinite period of time. This is contrasted with doing something about which you would feel good now but bad later with the bad being for an indefinite amount of time. In the M&M example discussed above, the individual turns down the M&M's and feels badly now; but later, perhaps much later when he achieves his goal to lose weight, feels good. The law of optional behavior applies to nearly all human activity because it causes us to process what we are doing and decide the long-term consequences of our behavior.

Coping with the law of optional behavior can have a dramatic impact on an individual's life. The most successful people have learned, and understand, the law of optional behavior and act in a manner which means the most to them in the long term. All of us, from time to time, seem to struggle through life without achieving some of our long term goals. At these times, we tend to act on basic impulses. At that time our behavior enables us to feel good first, but then bad later.

The law of optional behavior has much to do with achieving any goal we have set for ourselves. Financial goals, like other lifetime goals, can only be achieved by being disciplined and deferring immediate gratification for long term rewards.

Goal Setting

Setting realistic goals is the most important part of successful planning. But we do not establish goals in a vacuum. Our goals need to be based on our values and should be as specific as possible in the "how-to's." The process of setting goals is to ask ourselves "What is most important to me? Why? What do I need to do to achieve this goal?" These three questions help us clarify our thinking as to what is desirable for us in life and how to achieve it. Once we have identified our number one value, we ask "What is next most important to me?". By proceeding with this sequence of questions, we are able to prioritize our goals based on our values and put them into action. Chapters 13 and 14 have some detailed illustrations on these techniques. But first, we need to gain some understanding of the Eight Pathways.

CHAPTER 3
PATHWAY NO. ONE
CASH FLOW MANAGEMENT

Cash flow management is a process of monitoring the cash coming in and controlling the cash going out. The cash coming in is governed by how productive we are at our business or profession and how well our investments do. The cash we spend is controlled by establishing a budget and sticking to it.

Some people devote 100% of their effort in the cash flow management area to the cash coming in. They spend exhausting hours at work, agonize over investments, and then spend and consume with reckless abandon. These people need some balance. Every $1,000 we save ourselves through a disciplined budget is the equivalent of earning an additional $1,000. Because the world will impose limits on how much we can make, we must impose limits on how much we spend.

Three of the remaining pathways deal with investments, or sources of cash inflow. But unless we are retired and have been energetic savers, the greatest source of our cash inflow is from our business or profession, the proverbial golden goose.

The Golden Goose

Most of us make plans on the assumption that our jobs will not only continue indefinitely but will allow us yearly to earn more money. Yet, our advance in a given profession or business should not be taken as something the world owes us. It is something that takes hard work, continuing training, and trials and tribulations. Most of us are financially dependent on the economic rewards of our work. Our profession or business is the golden goose, and if the

14K
PETRIE

golden goose is killed, our financial plan will suddenly be completely out of wack.

Increases in earned income do not simply happen. The professional must strive to keep current with his area of expertise and must be prepared to redefine that area as conditions change. Each of us must think about where his profession is headed and what he is doing to be part of its future.

In his book *Million Dollar Profiles* (1958 - The Insurance Field Company, Inc.) William T. Earls, CLU profiled the lives of 27 of the most successful life insurance salesman of his area. He concluded that the key qualities to these 27 individuals were as follows:

1. Alert - They were attuned to current conditions, quick to move in and take advantage of changing business and tax trends that affected their business.
2. Willingness to Pay the Price - they were organized and worked long hours to make the most of the time available to them.
3. Integrity - Although each individual was very busy, each was a devoted family man, practicing member of some church,and a liberal contributor of time and talents to civic and business activities. They were attractive, honorable, outstanding sincere personalities and business leaders by any standards.

While Mr. Earls has since gone to his reward and his book for many years has been out of print, the characteristics that earmarked the successful life insurance agents in his day are characteristics that will stand the test of time for all different professionals and businessmen.

The Process of Vocational Growth

Although professions and business careers can require radically different skills, education and training, the process of becoming an outstanding achiever in one's career is very much the same for all vocations.

The process of superior achievement begins with the adoption of a role model. This role model can be a real person or it can be someone that we create as our ideal. Our role model is the person we would like to become as we grow in our career. Once we have this role model in mind, we then set a standard against which to compare, measure and guide our behavior. When in doubt as to what to do, we ask ourselves, "What would our role model do in this situation?" This process helps motivate creative thinking and frees us of our own internal dialogue which can lead to indecisiveness.

As an example, if I were to become a college basketball coach, I would read everything I could find on four of the all- time great coaches, John Wooden, Dean Smith, Bob Knight and Denny Crum. From this study I would put together a role model - a coach who would be a great recruiter, motivator, tactician and scintillating after dinner speaker. This ideal coach would be on the sidelines with me during practice and in the tight games.

Part of what the adoption of a role model motivates us to do is to strive for perfection. Now no one is ever going to achieve perfection, but by striving for it, we each can make considerable improvement in what we do. Lofty ideals and expections precede excellent performance. Although our performance will not always be perfect, it helps to aim for that level of excellence.

Another part of the process of superior achievement is to ask ourselves "What is expected of me in this situation?" To answer this question necessarily requires us to identify who we serve and what we are expected to do. Also, we can ask ourselves this question, "Are we doing more than what we are being paid to do?" If we are, we create a demand for our services and opportunity for future advancement. If we are not, we better begin.

Finally, no discussion of the golden goose would be complete without emphasizing the importance of being able to change and adapt. As John Naisbett has said in Megatrends, "In a world that is constantly changing, there is no one subject or set of subjects that will serve you for the foreseeable future, let alone for the rest of your life. The most important skill to acquire now is learning how to learn."

Advice From Mistakes

Life provides us with a constant source of growth opportunities. We each have different experiences and learn from them, whether we view them as productive or non-productive, and move on all the same. Some people appear to have found the ladder of success in their business. They start with one company or one profession and seem to do better and better each year. Others change jobs and careers as part of their success journey.

Whether you are one who is well situated with your current profession and job or one who is expecting to make a career change in the near future, you will continue to learn from your mistakes as well as from your successes. Although personal experience is generally the best teacher, we can also learn from the experiences of others.

Mistakes should be viewed as little more than a learning experience. If we never make a mistake, it is because we are not challenging ourselves enough. Mistakes simply teach us that we have something to learn, that next time we should do something different. In many respects, mistakes are the most productive learning experiences we can have.

The following are brief summaries of typical mistakes. If you haven't already had these particular learning experiences yourself, perhaps you can avoid them and move on to others.

1. Bradley was an assistant golf professional at a private club in southern Florida. He had an engaging personality and became friends with a couple of high rollers at his club who had struck it rich in real estate development. They were expanding their business so fast that they needed some help and persuaded Bradley to quit his job and come with them. A new condominium project was formulated and Bradley was asked to sign on the construction note as one of its partners in the development. He did so based on his friends' experience and recommendation rather than on his own understanding of real estate. When the condominium market slowed, cash flow became insufficient to carry the construction debt and Bradley, with his friends, had to default on the note. When last seen, Bradley was working as a bell boy in a resort hotel to pay off

some lingering debts.

2. Steve had a print shop that was very profitable. He had developed a niche in the marketplace and specialized in producing stationery for companies. As part of his strategy for the future, he decided to diversify and get into some areas of silk screening and engraving. He borrowed to purchase new equipment and expand his production staff. Up to this point in time his business had been financially straightforward - no real complication. But with the addition of new equipment and services, Steve had a need for sophisticated financial cost accounting, pricing and cash flow management - none of which he obtained until he had sustained massive losses. Steve not only got behind on bank payments but also owed money to the IRS on employer withholding taxes. When Steve went to the venture capital markets to attempt to bring in some capital, he found he had to give up control of his business in order to try to pull things out.

3. Oscar, age 62, owned a manufacturing representative business. He had one key employee, Ralph, age 35, whom Oscar treated well but who had never been permitted to become a shareholder. Oscar wanted to have some type of agreement that would permit him to sell the stock to Ralph when he chose to retire, but he did not want to be locked into a set retirement date. Nor did he want to make Ralph a shareholder before he retired from the business. Ralph wanted more certainty in his life and felt he was entitled to be a shareholder in the business. When Ralph's cloudy future did not become any clearer, he quit and began to compete directly with Oscar. Oscar not only wound up suing Ralph but also had to cultivate a relationship with another employee who would eventually enter into an agreement to purchase the business from Oscar.

4. Mr. C started his business career showing horses, expanded his business to include the building of high class carriages and was a potential player in the start up of the automobile industry. He was convinced Henry Ford could not use an assembly line to build cars. After all, cars or carriages had to be custom made and had to have baskets on both sides above the head lamps to hold flowers. When Henry Ford came out with the Model T, Mr. C was quickly buried by his competition.

5. Ed and Brenda were a young married couple with two children. Each was gainfully employed. In keeping with their 'station' as Yuppies they purchased a home in a fashionable neighborhood, financed two moderate to highly priced automobiles and led the good life on seven different credit cards. When financial stress among other things caused their marriage to become unglued, Ed was unable to keep up the child support and still pay on the credit cards. The house had to be sold at a loss because neither of the parties could afford the payment and the cars represented a burden to both parties. Because Ed and Brenda had developed a life style that consumed their entire earnings without any provision for savings or for meeting extraordinary costs, their readjustment to single life and as a single parent was made more difficult by the financial readjustment that was required. With two incomes and a relatively high salary, the problem could have been avoided by rudimentary cash flow management.

Budgeting

The fuel for the propulsion of a financial plan is the generation of savings. In order for there to be savings, there must be a budget and cash flow must be kept within that budget.

I have seen many clients with extraordinarily good incomes have an extraordinarily difficult time generating a net worth that is commensurate with their earning power. Net worth does not automatically come with high income but rather is something that is earned through conscientious savings and budgeting. The key to the wealth accumulation process is the periodic saving of money. Through savings, money can be made available for investment. Figure 3.1 sets forth the saving and investing of $1,000 per year at various compound interest rates. The message this chart should give you is that the earlier you begin to save, the better off you will be in the long run. Of course, a high interest rate also helps. But the advantage of high interest can be offset by high inflation so do not feel like you are being cheated by current low interest rates.

The process of setting a budget and sticking to it is an admirable

FIGURE 3.1
RESULT OF SAVING $1,000 PER YEAR AT VARIOUS AFTER-TAX INTEREST RATES

Year	06%	09%	12%	15%
1	1060	1090	1120	1150
2	2180	2280	2370	2470
3	3370	3570	3780	3990
4	4640	4980	5350	5740
5	5980	6520	7120	7750
6	7390	8200	9090	10070
7	8900	10030	11300	12730
8	10490	12020	13780	15790
9	12180	14190	16550	19300
10	13970	16560	19650	23350
11	15870	19140	23130	28000
12	17880	21950	27030	33350
13	20020	25020	31390	39500
14	22280	28360	36280	46580
15	24670	32000	41750	54720
16	27210	35970	47880	64080
17	29910	40300	54750	74840
18	32760	45020	62440	87210
19	35790	50160	71050	101440
20	38990	55760	80700	117810
21	42390	61870	91500	136630
22	46000	68530	103600	158280
23	49820	75790	117160	183170
24	53860	83700	132330	211790
25	58160	92320	149330	244710
26	62710	101720	168370	282570
27	67530	111970	189700	326100
28	72640	123140	213580	376170
29	78060	135310	240330	433750
30	83800	148580	270290	499960
31	89890	163040	303850	576100
32	96340	178800	341430	663670
33	103180	195980	383520	764370
34	110430	214710	430660	880170
35	118120	235120	483460	1013350
36	126270	257380	542600	1166500
37	134900	281630	608830	1342620
38	144060	308070	683010	1545170
39	153760	336880	766090	1778090
40	164050	368290	859140	2045950

and difficult task. Essentially, it requires identifying all monthly expenses and then each month checking the actual expenditures versus the budget. There are some people who by design will spend more than their earned income. These people are using investment income to allow a higher standard of living. There is absolutely nothing wrong with this approach, it is just that the approach must be understood and some limitations must be set on how much investment income will be consumed and how much will be saved. If investment principal is being consumed, financial problems may be looming on the horizon.

As we said earlier, without a sense of direction expenditures can run completely out of hand. A form allowing you to prepare a model budget is presented at the end of this Chapter for your use. Note that savings is the first expense item to be considered. After taxes and before expenses, part of whatever you make can be yours to keep.

While a strict budgeting process is probably the ideal, it is often not very practical for high powered people to spend significant amounts of time figuring out what their dry cleaning and gasoline expenses have been during a month's period. A more practical approach is for husband and wife each to have a monthly budget and to save and spend within the limits of each month's allowance. Whatever each saves can be spent in the future on a discretionary basis. This will not lead easily to large purchases such as a new automobile or expensive art work, but it does provide for some reference point for cash flow management. Also, it gives the couple some guidelines as to what their basic living expenses are on a month to month basis. Money available after the monthly allowances may be saved for either investment or for extraordinary expenses.

The Importance of Savings

John Templeton of the world famous Templeton Fund has said that everybody has at least one opportunity during their lifetime to make an extraordinarily good investment. Has your opportunity already come? If so, were you in a position to take advantage of it? Without systematic and adequate savings, none of us can ever accumulate much in the way of wealth, whether or not we are blessed with Mr. Templeton's once in a lifetime opportunity.

Savings are the cornerstone of individual financial planning and of capital formation in this country and abroad. It is no coincidence that what helps each of us achieve wealth during our lifetimes also helps others grow and prosper. Our personal savings and investments become available to businesses for purchases of new plants and equipment which can help increase the productivity of workers. In the true sense, the wealth of individuals can only increase as the wealth of the nation and the world increases. Without general increases in wealth, we play a zero sum game - an individual can gain wealth only as someone else loses it.

> It is my experience that most people try to live two years ahead of where they are; i.e. they buy based on their earnings over the next two years. If people will defer gratification and live two years behind their abilities, they will achieve the advantage of drawing rather than paying interest on money, and having a cushion if times go bad.
>
> — Robert A. Goering, Esq.
> Bankruptcy Attorney
> Cincinnati, Ohio

MONTHLY BUDGET SHEET

Here's a basic personal budget. Record yourmonthly income. Then figure your expenses - the combined total of all fixed and all flexible expenses. Finally, subtract expenses from income to determine your monthly balance. The way to a successful budget is to be realistic about income and expenses. Make savings your No. 1 and most important expense.

MONTHLY INCOME

Salary (gross)........ ________

Bonus (gross)........ ________

Interest........ ________

Dividends........ ________

Rental Income .... ________

Oil and Gas Royalties........ ________

Other .... ________

Alimony........ ________

Child Support .... ________

MONTHLY FIXED EXPENSES

Savings........ ________

Charitable Contributions........ ________

Taxes........ ________

IRA, Other Retirement .... ________

Child Care........ ________

Child Support .... ________

Alimony........ ________

House Payment or Rent........ ________

Second Mortgage .... ________

Motor Vehicle Loan........ ________

Other Loan .... ________

.... ________

Insurance (Home & Car)........ ________

Insurance (Health)........ ________

Insurance (Life) .... ________

Insurance (Disability) .... ________

Other .... ________

Subtotal .... ________

MONTHLY FLEXIBLE EXPENSES

Household .... ________

Utilities........ ________

Telephone .... ________

Cable TV .... ________

Other .... ________

.... ________

Groceries (Home)........ ________

Restaurants, Carryout .... ________

Lunches (Work)........ ________

Medicine........ ________

Cosmetics........ ________

Other .... ________

Car (Gas, Oil & Repairs)........ ________

Parking........ ________

Bus, Taxi, Train Fares........ ________

Other Transportation .... ________

Visa .... ________

Other .... ________

.... ________

Newspapers........ ________

Magazines, Books........ ________

Sports, Movies, Etc........ ________

Tobacco, Candy, Etc........ ________

Vacations........ ________

Other Entertainment .... ________

.... ________

Tuition .... ________

Textbooks........ ________

Other .... ________

.... ________

Clothes & Shoes .... ________

Accessories .... ________

Laundry, Dry Cleaning .... ________

Beauty Shop, Barber .... ________

Gifts, Birthdays, Etc. .... ________

Allowances .... ________

Medical (Doctors) .... ________

Dentist........ ________

.... ________

Master Card........ ________

Other .... ________

.... ________

.... ________

Subtotal .... ________

Subtotal, Fixed Expenses.. ________
(From above)

TOTALEXPENSES........ ________

BALANCING YOUR BUDGET

Total Income........ ________

Total Expenses........ ________

Balance........ ________

CHAPTER 4
PATHWAY NO. TWO
INSURANCE MATTERS

The purchase of insurance may seem like one of the least exciting parts of financial planning, but it is one of the most important. Without insurance, all of our planning, expectations and dreams can be wiped out by a serious illness, disability or death.

The purchase of adequate insurance protection is a passage to other investment opportunities. Without adequate insurance, it makes little sense for an individual to plan for retirement or to be concerned about balance in his investment portfolio.

Why Life Insurance

Life insurance is the best investment ever created from a tax standpoint. The proceeds at death are paid to the named beneficiary on a tax free basis except for transfer for value situations discussed below. The accumulation of cash value within the policy occurs on a tax-free basis until such time, if ever, as the policy is surrendered. With all policies purchased prior to July 1, 1984, most policies purchased prior to January 1, 1985, and on many purchased thereafter, partial surrenders can be made, up to the cost of the contract, on a tax free basis. With all policies except some single premium whole life, loans can be made on a tax free basis. As explained in Pathway Number Eight (estate planning), life insurance can be owned in an irrevocable trust so that it is kept out of both an individual's estate and his or her spouse's estate. Let's now look at some of the income tax aspects of life insurance policies in more detail.

For those of us who are concerned about how our loved ones

would fare in this world without us, life insurance provides the opportunity to create an instant estate. With a stroke of a pen and a very small premium, a very large estate can be left to loved ones without that estate having to pass through the income tax wringer. One exception to the tax free payment of the proceeds occurs when the policy is sold or otherwise transferred during the holder's lifetime for valuable consideration. This so-called transfer-for-value rule does not apply in the case of certain important exceptions, such as the transfer of ownership of an insurance policy to the insured. Nevertheless, you should consult your tax advisor or life insurance agent before you attempt to change the beneficiary or owner of a policy in any situation in which you receive some value for making a change. A gift of a policy to a spouse or into trust is not a transfer for value. The only other exception to the tax free payment of life insurance proceeds is when a third party owner exists. For example, if you are the insured on a life insurance policy and your wife is owner of the policy and she names a child beneficiary, at your death the insurance company pays the proceeds to your child and, since your wife was owner of the policy, this forms a gift from her to your child. Even though the proceeds are received income tax free by your child, gift taxes may be due on the gift if the policy is larger than the annual $10,000 your wife could gift to a child without tax. To eliminate the above mentioned problem, simply make sure no third party owner is involved. If the owner is the beneficiary then no tax liability will exist.

The cash value accumulation on a whole life or universal life insurance contract occurs income tax free. Tax free accumulation has often been subject to some extensive discussion under tax laws considered by Congress but there appears to be no change on the horizon--in large part thanks to the intensive lobbying of the insurance industry. The cash value accumulation of a life insurance contract is readily available to the policyholder, albeit subject to possible income tax consequences. He can either borrow the cash value at a fixed rate such as six to eight percent in many contracts (or at what may be a significantly higher rate if a variable rate is used in an interest sensitive policy) or he can obtain the cash value of the policy upon surrender of it to the insurance company.

Because of the new tax laws, interest paid by individuals on borrowings from insurance policies will no longer be deductible with phase-out occurring over a five year period. Income taxes may have to be paid upon the surrender of the policy, but only if the cash value is in excess of the premiums paid. This would generally not happen for six or seven years with most typical life insurance contracts since a significant portion of each premium is used for the pure term insurance coverage and early premiums are used to pay for front end costs. For policies purchased after December 31, 1984, any partial surrender of the contract within the first 15 years may be subject to income tax to the extent of income in the contract. This generally would happen only with policies which have a cash value which is close to the maximum allowed for the current death benefit of the contract. Also, it is possible that borrowings from certain single premium whole life policies that provide a net zero interest on borrowings will be treated as partial surrenders and subject to tax. Check with your insurance or tax advisor before making a loan, a withdrawal or any partial surrender of your insurance policy.

Many people today are purchasing a single premium whole life or a single premium universal life policy for the tax advantage of the investment in the life insurance policy. When you consider that most major insurance companies are paying two to three percent higher than money market rates in a falling interest environment and no less than current money market rates in an increasing interest environment, and that this interest inside the policy is currently not taxed, it becomes apparent that a life insurance policy can be a very attractive place to stash safe money. However, it was not the intent of Congress to create a tax free current investment vehicle with a life insurance policy. Therefore, if insurance policies continue to be marketed as tax free income vehicles, Congress will probably act to correct this abuse. The withdrawal and loan provisions of life insurance contracts were intended for use in an emergency and not as periodic tax free income; but you should probably not forego the purchase of an insurance policy because the law may be changed in the future. In most cases current provisions would be "grandfathered" in the event of future changes in the tax treatment of loans and withdrawals. Thus a law change could simply make insurance policies purchased now more valuable than ever.

Types of Life Insurance

There have been some dramatic changes in the life insurance industry in recent years. As a result, consumers have more policies from which to choose and more opportunity to make the purchase of life insurance both an investment as well as the purchase of protection for loved ones. Let's now take a look at the various types of life insurance policies.

Term insurance is the most basic type of insurance and simply provides for the purchase of pure death benefit protection. Term insurance rates are based on your health and your age. The longer you hold a term policy after satisfying the physical requirements, the higher the cost will be because of the increased uncertainties of your current health status.

In the last several years, insurance companies have designed term policies which make it attractive to requalify for your existing term. Consequently, insurance agents have been suggesting that you replace your insurance with a new policy from a different company every other year. This practice is very unprofitable to insurance companies. Therefore, you may find that the technique will not be possible the next time you switch companies, as major companies are beginning to refuse new coverage on anyone who has switched insurance three times in the past five years.

Whole life insurance combines pure death benefit protection with an investment feature. The investment part of the contract is called the cash surrender value. Because you are both making an investment and purchasing pure death benefit protection, you will pay significantly more in the beginning in premium for whole life insurance than for term insurance. Whole life insurance generally requires the payment of a fixed premium each year although it is possible to borrow from existing cash value to pay the premiums. Also, whole life policies can be designed so the policyholder can pay up the policy over a period of time, such as 10 years, and not have to make any additional premium payments. If you purchase a whole life policy from a mutual insurance company (a company owned by its policyholders) or a stock company which issues a participating policy, you will receive dividends each year. These "dividend" payments are considered a refund of an overpayment in premiums and are therefore tax free. On the other hand, if you purchase a whole life policy from a stock insurance company which issues non-participating policies, your cash surrender value will simply be credited with tax deferred interest each year. You cannot measure the quality of an insurance contract by whether it is issued by a mutual or stock company. The way an insurance company is managed is the most important criterion to the overall competitiveness of its insurance policies.

Universal life insurance is similar to whole life in that it combines an investment feature with pure death benefit protection. However, universal life provides for flexibility in the premiums that are paid as well as in the amount of death benefit provided under the contract. There is a further discussion of universal life under the section of this chapter titled "The New Wave of Life Insurance Policies."

Both whole life and universal life can be single premium policies which means only one premium is paid. Also, both types of insurance policies can provide for investment of the cash value in different investment mediums, such as stocks, bonds, real estate, or money market accounts. This type of insurance is called "variable whole life" or "variable universal life." *Because variable life insurance permits an individual to invest in the stock market without any current income tax consequences, it is becoming an increasingly popular product.*

The last statement requires some elaboration. For several years many insurance agents have suggested that an individual buy term insurance and invest the difference in investments which have a potential for higher returns, such as mutual funds. In fact, a few companies use this approach as their primary marketing theme. It is important you understand the taxation of "buy term and invest the difference". We will then discuss how a variable life insurance contract provides an attractive alternative.

The purchase of term insurance and the investment are both made with your after-tax dollars. Since this approach assumes that there is only a temporary need for insurance, (e.g., while you have small children, a mortgage, etc.) at some point in time, say age 65, the term insurance becomes so expensive that you no longer pay the premium. At this point, it is assumed that your difference has been regularly invested in a high yield investment and you have so much money that you no longer "need" the insurance. This sounds good, but let's examine the tax consequences. Assume that you have had an average of one hundred dollars per month to invest over a 30 year period. Let's further assume that in the beginning you spend $20 per month for $100,000 of low cost term insurance and you invest $80 in a good family of mutual funds. We will also assume that the cost of the term insurance will increase by $10 per month once each five years from age 35 to age 65. Therefore in the last five years you are allocating $70 to insurance and $30 to the mutual fund investment. If we assume an average rate of growth in the mutual fund of 10%, you will accumulate $146,060 by age 65. Along the way you will pay ordinary income tax on the dividends received from the mutual fund, (even though you reinvested in the fund) which reduces the fund's compound growth from 11% compounded to 10%. During this 30 year period of time, suppose the Dow Industrials Index goes from 9,000 to 36,000, and there are at least five major up and down cycles in the market.

At this point you may be feeling great about buying term and investing the difference. You will outperform a typical whole life insurance policy and will accumulate a nice nest egg to use to supplement your retirement income if needed. You could withdraw $14,606 each year - the entire growth from your fund (assuming the balance continues to earn 10%) - for the 20 years from age 65 to age 85 when you die. Since you did not sell your mutual fund over the years, you will have deferred the income taxes on the increase in value of the account. But you must pay 33% taxes on the income of $14,985 so your net income is $9,786 after taxes. At your death the balance of $146,060 is included in your estate for federal estate tax purposes and your heirs will receive a step up in basis which means your mutual fund can be sold at your death without generating any more income taxes.

On the other hand, if you had invested in a variable life insurance policy, and taken essentially the same investment risk, your situation would be very different. First, all earnings would have been tax deferred including dividend payments. Also, if you had been smart enough to switch from common stocks, inside the insurance contract, to the money market account during the 5 or 6 major down markets over the 30 years of investing, you would not have had to pay income taxes on any of these transactions as you would have had to in the comparative mutual fund. If because of these two major tax advantages, you increase your rate of accumulation by only 2% over the life of the investment, your cash accumulation at age 65 would be $237,852 instead of $146,060 in the mutual fund, and you would still have the $100,000 of life insurance payable to your beneficiary in addition to the $237,852 of cash accumulation. So if death occurs at age 65 your beneficiary will receive $337,852 income tax free instead of $146,060. On the other hand, if you begin withdrawing $14,985 from the insurance policy, under current tax law, you will not pay any income taxes. Therefore your after tax income will be increased from $9,786 to $14,985. If you live for 11 years and die, your beneficiary will receive $515,657 in tax free death proceeds instead of the principal of $146,060 in the mutual fund. This is why so many people are sold on variable universal life as the policy of the future. It certainly appears to be a much stronger program from a tax standpoint than "buy term and invest the difference."

The Purchase of Life Insurance

The purchase of life insurance is a four step process. The first step is making the decision as to how much life insurance to purchase; the second step is deciding what type of life insurance (term or whole life or universal life) to purchase; the third step is deciding how the life insurance is owned; the fourth step is naming the beneficiary.

a. How much insurance to purchase

In order to calculate the amount of insurance that you need, you need to make the following decisions:

1. What interest rate do you think can be earned on your insurance proceeds--assume 10%.

2. What do you think the rate of inflation will be in the future--assume 5%.

3. How much income do you want your family to receive in the event of your death--assume $50,000.

4. What other liquidity will you have available other than insurance proceeds--assume $200,000.

The formula for determining the amount of insurance that you need is:

(1-2) x (insurance coverage + 4) = 3.

Let's take a look at what this formula means. Essentially, this formula proposes you purchase enough insurance coverage so that coupled with your other liquid assets, you can take the assumed rate of return (here 10%) on your insurance proceeds plus liquidity, pay out to your family the cash needed on a current basis as income, and take the excess and add it back to your principal. This enables you to have an income stream which will grow each year to keep pace with inflation. The beauty of this formula is that if inflation increases, the rate of return will also increase so that you should be able to provide a fairly constant income to keep pace with the inflation changes.

In the above example, the total insurance needed would be $800,000. The insurance proceeds coupled with the other liquid investments would provide a return of $50,000 per year of income to the family and allow an additional $50,000 to be added to principal. In the second year, there would then be a total of $52,500 with another $52,500 added to the principal and so on. A work sheet is included at the end of this chapter for you to make your own calculation.

If this results in the purchase of more insurance than you would otherwise feel necessary, then you may need to examine your assumptions and needs. It certainly is possible that the inflation rate will not be 5% as we look forward--it could be lower, it could be higher. It is also possible that you would want your family to consume principal so that there would not be a constant growth in principal. However, if this happens you need to make some predictions about your family's life expectancy and this involves some risk taking.

Another way to approximate the amount of life insurance needed is to make sure that interest on the life insurance proceeds (plus other investment assets) would replace the insured's earned income. In other words, if an individual has $100,000 of earned income each year, he should be covered by $1,000,000 of insurance (assuming 10% interest can be earned on the insurance proceeds and no other investment assets). The National Insurance Consumer Organization recommends for families with two or more children to have total life insurance protection equal to six times the insured's annual income.

Of course, the amount of life insurance an individual should own is governed by what other assets he has. If an individual has significant other liquid assets, the need for life insurance to provide assets in the event of death is reduced. On the other hand, if an individual has a very large estate that will necessitate the payment of estate taxes, life insurance may be needed to assist in providing liquidity for the payment of death taxes.

b. What type to purchase

Once you have decided the amount of life insurance to purchase, you must decide what type of insurance to purchase.

Term insurance, which provides a death benefit only, is usually the type of insurance you should initially purchase. Term is more affordable in that it cost less in the early years and by purchasing term it is more likely that you will acquire sufficient insurance coverage. Young people should consider purchasing more term insurance then they currently need, just to protect insurability. Protecting your insurability can make this an excellent investment.

Under what circumstances should you consider buying whole life or universal life insurance instead of term insurance to provide for your life insurance needs? You should consider the purchase of whole life or universal life insurance when you can afford the additional premium payments and when any of the following factors exist: 1) you have difficulty saving money and would use the whole life or universal life contract to discipline yourself into saving more dollars; 2) you can find some entity (such as your corporation or qualified plan) to pay for the additional premium so that you can eventually obtain ownership of the policy after the front end costs (commissions and insurance company administrative costs) have been paid; 3) you anticipate holding onto the policy for a long time and like the idea of a level premium; 4) you have attained an advanced age and the cost of term insurance will become more expensive than the whole life coverage in a very few years; 5) you are in a high tax bracket and the tax free accumulation of cash values is attractive to you; or 6) you have a lump sum of safe cash which you are free to invest and which is currently being taxed. If any of the above factors exist, you should consider the purchase of whole life or universal life insurance. In any event, do not hesitate to consult with your accountant, attorney or insurance professional for their advice.

c. Ownership

Ownership needs to be determined after the amount and type of life insurance policy is selected. Typically the insured is the owner unless for federal estate tax reasons a child or an irrevocable trust is named as owner. If a policy is purchased in connection with a business, the owner may be the company or an individual other than the insured if the insurance is purchased to fund a buy sell agreement.

In the corporate setting, a whole life or universal life policy can be purchased on a split dollar basis. In the most typical case, the employee is the insured under the policy and splits the cost of the insurance with his employer. The employer pays for the bulk of the premiums and the employee pays for the pure death benefit cost of the policy, referred to as PS 58 cost. The employee generally owns the policy but assigns it to the employer as security for the premiums the employer has advanced. The employer is generally guaranteed a return of the lesser of premiums paid or the cash surrender value of the policy. In this way, at the death of the insured, the corporation is repaid part or all of what it has paid into the policy. The split dollar contract is a very advantageous way of purchasing life insurance since it utilizes corporate money on essentially an interest free basis.

d. Beneficiary

If the insured is the owner, he needs to name someone else as beneficiary. Typically he would cause the life insurance proceeds to be received by a trust if that is part of his estate plan. It doesn't do any good to have a marital deduction trust set up for the ownership of life insurance if the spouse, rather than the trust, is named as beneficiary, because the terms of the contract will override any other provision regarding the life insurance. If someone other than the insured is the owner, that person usually must be the beneficiary.

The New Wave of Life Insurance Policies

Universal life insurance was the beginning of some very significant changes in the life insurance industry. Universal life provides for flexibility both in premium payments as well as in benefit coverage, *and in many respects may be the only policy that an individual needs for life.* Universal life has become extremely popular because the consumer has discovered that it is an excellent savings vehicle. A word of caution is in order especially for those who already own whole life policies. Computer illustrations are part of every sales pitch for universal life. Computer illustrations can make any life insurance program into a spectacular performer over a long period of time assuming that high interest rates can be paid by insurance companies. Do not trash all your existing whole life policies in favor of universal life just because the computer tells you to do so. Be sure that you understand that what you are giving up may represent an attractive insurance program because you may have already paid for the front end costs. There are many whole life programs that can benefit from a universal life overhaul; there are also some that should be kept in place and not changed.

With universal life insurance and other types of interest sensitive life insurance products, computer illustrations are used to predict the future of the cash value accumulations. Yet, any computer illustration must make assumptions about long term interest rates that the insurance company will credit to the cash values of insurance policies. Clearly an insurance company can not continue to credit high returns on cash values if its portfolio of investments does not yield a return significantly in excess of those returns. Stated another way, if a life insurance company's portfolio return is lagging behind what it promises to credit on cash values, it is unlikely the high interest promised will be credited for very long. Yet, many companies are illustrating interest rates on new money that are in excess of the rates of return they earn on their investment portfolios

The high interest rates offered on any new universal life or whole life product can be used to encourage sales but mean very little about the product's future. Consequently, the investor should buy life insurance from a company that he believes will be able to remain competitive in any interest environment with diversified wise investments over a long period of time and internal expense controls, and not from a company which simply offers the highest interest today on cash values.

Second-to-die life insurance policies are a very attractive way to provide liquidity for the payment of estate taxes. The second-to-die policies produce the dollars when needed, at the second death of husband and wife. It is imperative that these policies be either owned by an irrevocable insurance trust or someone other than either insured, such as a child, in order to maximize the favorable tax advantages.

Single Premium Whole Life

Single premium whole life could have been discussed in the low-risk, low-return investment chapter of this book since it is as much an investment product as it is a life insurance product. However, a single premium whole life policy does require a certain amount of life insurance protection. Outside of that factor, the policy looks more like a single premium deferred annuity than like a typical life insurance contract. The reason for this is that it provides for the compounding of interest within the policy. In addition, the commissions paid on a single premium life insurance policy are very low, similar to those paid on a single premium deferred annuity and for that reason there is not heavy loading. Thus, every dollar that goes into the policy is reflected as part of the cash value on which interest is credited. Single premium whole life can be an acceptable alternative to municipal bond purchases and can be a valuable part of an investment portfolio. Its back end surrender charges are similar to those of single premium deferred annuity products. This should not present a drawback if the insurance is properly purchased. Generally, a life insurance policy should be held until the death of the insured to maximize its tax advantage.

Single premium whole life is a life insurance product and as such is subject to continuing review by Congress. One of the aspects of single premium whole life which has been under attack is the aspect of many policies that has enabled policyholders to borrow from the policy with essentially no net charges (the so-called "wash loan"). Congress will not allow this to continue indefinitely.

Be sure that your agent brings you completely up to date on the tax effects of single premium whole life before you make it part of your investment and life insurance portfolio. Keep in mind that withdrawals from a single premium policy during the first 15 years may result in taxable income. This same rule may apply to "so called" wash loans. The reason I say "so called" wash loans is that these features are priced into the policy by the insurance companies issuing the policy. If a policy has a "wash loan" and the policy-owner exercise this option, the ultimate interest rate will be reduced to reflect this additional cost to the company. On policies where there is at least a 2% net cost to the loan the these policies will be able to pay higher interest rates and should in the long run perform equal to a "so called" wash loan. If loans are allowed to continue in the future it is my opinion that the net cost loan is the only concept that may survive the lawmaker axe.

Loans on Existing Policies

Interest on borrowing to purchase whole life insurance is not deductible. Also, pay special attention to the exchange of policies containing loans for new policies that do not contain loans. You may create taxable income to yourself. One policy may be exchanged for another on a tax-free basis under IRC §1035, but if a policy that has gain (cash value in excess of premiums paid) and an outstanding loan is canceled, the gain must be reported as income to the extent of the lesser of the loan or the gain.

Split Dollar of Purchase of Insurance

Life insurance can be purchased in a tax and cost efficient manner by use of a split dollar agreement with a corporation or other business entity. Typically the policy is owned by an individual or trust and collaterally assigned to the corporation as security for funds advanced by the corporation as its share of premium payments.

In a collateral assignment split dollar, the majority of the premium is paid by the corporation with the owner of the policy paying a small portion of the premium called the P.S. 58 costs which is the cost of the pure death benefit protection. The P.S. 58 cost is a table published by the Internal Revenue Service but usually a lower rate is used that is published by the insurance company relating to the cost of its term insurance product.

There are several advantages to split-dollar insurance. First, corporate dollars can be used for the premium payments. Corporate dollars in a regular corporation are taxed at only a 15% rate up to the first $50,000 so these dollars can represent less expensive dollars. In addition, for people who are purchasing the insurance in an irrevocable trust for estate planning purposes, the portion paid by the grantors of the trust is limited to the P.S. 58 cost (or, if lower, the cost of term coverage) thereby increasing the amount of insurance that can be purchased by contributions to the trust. This technique works especially well with second to die policies where the cost that applies to the pure death benefit is exceptionally low because of two lives being covered.

> **Example:** Richard and his wife Jean establish an irrevocable trust where they name an independent trustee, Oscar. Oscar applies for $5 million of second-to-die insur-

ance with Richard and Jean as insured and sets up a split-dollar agreement with Richard's corporation. Richard's corporation pays $100,000 of premiums for ten (10) years and Richard and Jean pay a very small premium attributable to the cost of the pure death benefit. At the end of the fifteen (15) years, the policy has enough in cash values that the million dollars advanced by the corporation is repaid and Richard and his wife now have a policy for the benefit of their children that has been paid for with assistance from the corporation. The $5 million insurance proceeds are received income and estate tax free upon the second death of Richard and Jean. If desired, Richard and Jean could have set up the irrevocable trust for the benefit of grandchildren.

While split-dollar arrangements are very popular, extreme care needs to be taken in the drafting of the split-dollar contract so that the corporation has no incidents of ownership. Otherwise, an unnecessary federal estate tax obligation can be created upon the death of the insured.

Disability Insurance

It is more likely that you will become disabled sometime before age 65 than that you will die before age 65. Because disability is not an infrequent phenomenon, you should have disability insurance to protect you and your family in the event of your disability. The cost of disability insurance varies dramatically from product to product. In addition the cost varies based on how long a waiting period must occur before the disability product kicks in as well on as how long the disability payments will run. If your family is solely dependent on your working for its welfare, you should consider buying a disability policy which will provide payments to you up until at least age 65 in the event of your disability.

There are many different disability products that are written. Be certain that you buy a product that will pay disability in the event that you are unable to perform the current responsibilities of your occupation--not just are unable to do any job at all. There are some disability policies which are written so broadly that if you are able to perform any work at all, you will not receive any benefits from the policy. Also, determine the cost of a noncancelable policy that will pay benefits to age 65 or beyond. This type of policy has a fixed premium and coverage can not be canceled as long as the premiums are paid. I recommend a disability policy with some form of inflation protection because once you are disabled a level income is better than no income at all, but an increasing income is even better.

Health Insurance

With the skyrocketing costs of medical care, it is vitally important that you keep your health insurance program up to date. Whether you are self-insured or insured through your employer, make certain that your major medical health insurance program covers your spouse and dependents. In addition, if you are maintaining your own health insurance, look into a program that has a higher deductible. Some insurance companies are charging outrageous amounts for first dollar protection, and in many cases it is advantageous to be self-insured to the extent of a large deductible.

Insurance companies change their health insurance premiums on a regular basis. Therefore, do not be shy about frequently asking your insurance agent to give you a new quote on what health insurance companies charge for various programs. If you own your own company and have a number of employees, you might look at a self-insured program or a shared funding program to minimize health insurance costs. This option usually works best only if you have 50 employees or more.

Property and Casualty Insurance

In order to have the proper coverage for property and casualty insurance, you need to have the services of an agent who is skilled in that area. You need to know what your different risks are and the type and amount of coverage that is recommended. Do not rely on your life insurance agent since most life insurance agents are not experts in property and casualty insurance. Generally, your life insurance agent should recommend an expert to you to handle your casualty and property insurance needs.

Be certain that you have adequate coverage for liability arising from your use and ownership of your automobile since jury awards are becoming increasingly out of sight. In addition, you probably should purchase an umbrella policy to provide some additional protection for unforeseen events.

INSURANCE CALCULATION

Amount of Insurance to Purchase
A = Rate of return projected for liquid assets
B = Rate of inflation
C = amount of other liquid assets
I = amount of insurance required to achieve objectives
Y = yearly income desired for family in event of death

$(A - B) \times (C + I) = Y$
$I = Y / (A - B) - C$

Fill in your own values for the above variables and solve the equation for the amount of insurance you should own.

I = Y ______________/ (A ________ - B _________) - C ________

With regard to what type of insurance to purchase, first be certain that you are purchasing enough insurance coverage (such as term). Then, if you choose to pay more for insurance than you have to because of age, tax brackets, or investment concerns, purchase whole life or universal life from a company that has demonstrated an ability to pay a consistently fair, high return on cash value accumulations with reasonable mortality costs. Also, find a product that has reasonable loading charges.

CHAPTER 5
PATHWAY NO. THREE CONSERVATIVE INVESTMENTS

The following three chapters will discuss the types of investments that should be in most portfolios. The concept behind a balanced investment program is that a diversified program will provide a positive yield in the long run regardless what happens to the economy. Many will tell you that they have had tremendous success putting all of their eggs in one basket and that the only way to go is real estate, oil and gas, stocks and bonds, etc. Nevertheless, on a percentage basis, these people are in the minority. Generally people who have not diversified have not had the kind of success which they could have had over a long period of time with a balanced portfolio.

The Importance of Diversification

The types of investments which we will cover will be low-risk, low-return; moderate-risk, moderate-return; and high-risk, high-return. Investments are classified in this manner to provide for protection of both principal and investment return for changes in the economy that can be attributable to changes in the following: rate of inflation, interest rates, stock market value, value of real estate, value of gold and other precious metals, and energy costs. If you could tell an insurance agent when you will die, he could tell you with great confidence what life insurance program you should have and help you obtain excellent results. By the same token, if you could tell an investment advisor what is going to happen with the economy, he could easily structure an investment program that would match that situation. However, no-one has 20/20 foresight, and the best any of us can do is to use our best judgment to invest in a manner that we think will be the most beneficial in the long run.

It does not make sense for us to become too committed to any one investment approach. We are better off if we balance our investment program and monitor the results of that balance. Of course, any investment program must allow for individual differences. I may think it is wise to have 20% of my money in real estate investments and you may choose to have 10% or 40% but probably not zero or 60%. Diversification is important for all of us.

Measuring Your Tolerance to Risk

There are a number of factors that affect an individual's tolerance for risk. Clearly a retiree with limited resources has a much lower tolerance for risk than a young professional whose income is on the rise. Factors that should be considered are age, stability of income, possible inheritances, and amount of money to invest currently versus expected yearly savings.

As a general rule, your investment dollars should be spread pretty evenly across the three general categories of investment. However, there may be factors in your life which would cause you to be more conservative or more aggressive than this general rule.

A worksheet is included at the end of this chapter to help you measure your tolerance to risk. If you score high (above 40), you may want to have a higher percentage of your assets in moderate risk and high risk investments than would otherwise be indicated. On the other hand, a low score indicates you should have the vast majority of your investment dollars in conservative and perhaps moderate risk investments.

Some investment advisers suggest that investments be made based on an investment triangle such as is presented in Figure 5.1. Low risk, low return are at the bottom of the triangle; moderate risk, moderate return at the middle; and high risk, high return at the top. The investment triangle presents several concepts. One is to first develop your foundation of low risk, low return investments before moving on to riskier investments. Second is to limit your riskier investments to a mere fraction of your more fundamental, solid type investments. Importantly, the size of the investments made in each section of the investment triangle are dependent on the investor's tolerance to risk so it is still useful to work through the exercise presented at the end of this chapter.

Figure 5.1
INVESTMENT TRIANGLE

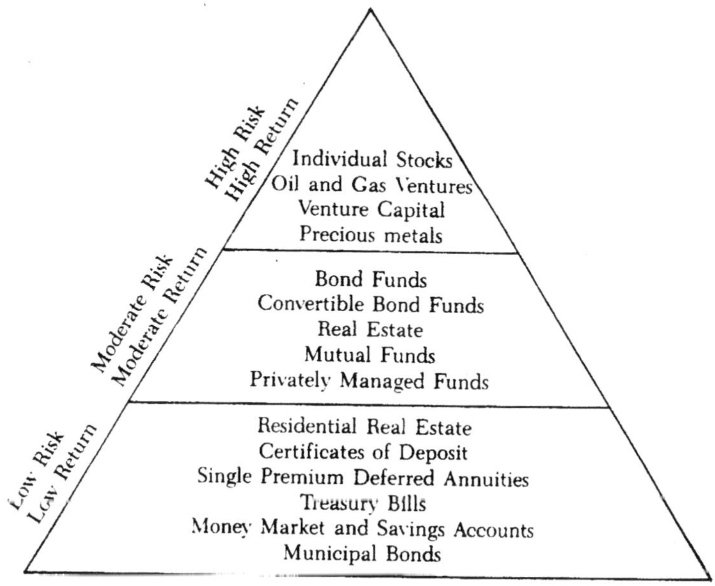

Low-Risk, Low-Return Investments In General

The concept of a low-risk, low-return investment does not mean that the rate of return will be low in comparison to all other investments. It does mean that your principal is safe and there probably is not a great chance for a high return. In most cases, if there is a upward tick in interest rates, the low-risk, low-return investment will suffer. Consequently, most low-risk, low-return investments do not fare well in an inflationary time and simply provide for a positive yield on assets which in the long run may or may not significantly outpace inflation. On the other hand, a decline in interest rates generally results in the appreciation of a low-risk, low-return investment.

Municipal Bonds

A tax favored investment which belongs in the category of low-risk, low-return is municipal bonds. A tax-free municipal bond earns income that is income tax free at the federal level and, if approved by the state in which the individual files his state tax return, will probably also be tax-free at the municipal and state level. The advantage of municipal bonds is simply that they do provide for a fairly good rate of return on a tax-free basis and, because of that, can outpace taxable investments which earn a much higher rate of return. The problem with tax-free municipal bonds is that if interest rates go up, the value of the underlying bond can decrease considerably. For example, when interest rates increased so dramatically in the late 1970's, a number of people who had purchased municipal bonds providing for a four, five, and six percent rate of return, found that their principle investment had lost significant value simply because comparable bonds were paying a much higher rate of return.

Generally, municipal bonds do not provide for a compound rate of return since most people who buy municipal bonds are looking for a current income stream to supplement their other income. However, zero coupon municipal bonds do provide for compounding of interest. To the extent that an individual has significant cash to invest for the future, and does not need current cash flow, zero coupon municipal bonds are an attractive investment. One client purchased a zero coupon municipal bond for $30,000 in 1985 which will mature for $800,000 in the year 2015. This is deferred gratification!

If an individual chooses to invest in municipal bonds, it is desirable to have those municipal bond purchases spread out over a number of different issues. We only have to look back on the Washington Public Power Supply System's $2.25 billion bond default to appreciate that the safety of a municipal bond is not guaranteed. There are also municipal bond funds, some of which are insured. If you buy municipal bonds, check whether the bonds are callable. If they are callable, your principal may be returned to you before the due date of the bond. This happens when interest rates decrease markedly after bonds are issued. Also, you can find municipal bonds which are guaranteed. This means collateral covers the bond and you have virtually no risk in getting a return of your principal.

Government Securities

There are a number of different ways to invest in government securities. Treasury bills offer the simplest way of investing at zero-risk and low-return. Since interest is paid and taxed when the bills mature, the purchase of treasury bills can be timed so that the interest received will be taxed in a later year. Zero coupon treasury bonds provide for the compounding of interest over a period of time and can be placed in a child's portfolio so as to guarantee significant, lightly taxed money for college education.

It is also possible to invest in mortgage-backed securities through mutual funds. These mutual funds provide for rates of return as much as one percent higher than Treasuries, but are inter est sensitive and can cause a real erosion in an individual's invested principal if there is a large fluctuation in interest rates. Also, since the mortgages held by these funds may be prepaid if the borrower can refinance at lower interest rates, the investor may come up with a liquidating fund which does not provide the return expected over the period expected. Only the principal is guaranteed by the feds, not the rate of return.

There are a number of different types of mortgage-backed securities. Each has its own features and appeals to different types of investors. The largest group of mortgage-backed securities is known as "Pass-Throughs" because mortgage interest and principal payments are "passed through" a servicing institution to investors. All pass-throughs are similar in structure and share common characteristics. There are three basic types: Government National

Mortgage Association or GNMA: Federal National Mortgage Association or FNMA; and Federal Home Loan Mortgage Corporation or FHLMC.

The Government National Mortgage Association, or "Ginnie Mae," guarantees their pass-through securities with the full faith and credit of the U.S. government. Because of their safety, Ginnie Maes are appropriate for a wide variety of investors. They are the most liquid type of pass-through, representing over one-half of all pass-throughs outstanding.

The second type of mortgage-backed security is from the Federal National Mortgage Association, or "Fannie Mae." FNMA is a privately held corporation but maintains federal agency status and has a very large credit line with the U.S. Treasury. Fannie Mae guarantees timely payment of principal and interest on its pass-through securities. Fannie Maes are liquid and usually trade in the secondary market at higher yields than Ginnie Maes.

The third type of pass-through is from the Federal Home Loan Mortgage Corporation, or "Freddie Mac." This institution was established by Congress in 1970, is owned by the 12 member banks of the Federal Home Loan Bank System, and has federal agency status. FHLMC guarantees the timely payment of interest and ultimate payment of principal. This means that it will pass through whatever principal it collects and guarantees the remainder within a year. Pass-throughs are a very popular form of mortgage-backed security.

Besides the different types of pass-throughs, there are additional mortgage-backed securities for you to consider. Probably the most important are builder bonds. Builder bonds are mortgage-backed securities issued by some of the nation's largest home builders. Builders offer mortgages to qualified home buyers through their own financing subsidiaries. These mortgage are then converted into Ginnie Maes or Fannie Maes which are used as collateral for the builder bonds. Proceeds from the builder bond issue are available to the builder for the construction of more homes.

EE bonds offer perhaps the most attractive means of purchasing a "guaranteed" investment. These bonds are backed by the full faith and credit of the U.S. government. No commission or fee is involved in the purchase of the bonds, the return is variable in that it can rise as market interest rates increase, and the holding period can be extended beyond the EE bond's 10 year limit by rolling the funds over into HH bonds in a nontaxable event. The variable interest rate is set every six months at 85% of the average yield (for the prior six months) on five-year Treasury bills. The EE bonds may be purchased for as little as $25 or as much as $5,000, with a limit of $15,000 per taxpayer per year. These bonds serve as an excellent investment for under age 14 children's funds because no tax is due on income accruing on the bonds until they are redeemed.

HH bonds can serve as a retirement annuity, with taxes due only on semi-annual interest payments. The increase in principal earned by the EE bonds remains tax-deferred as only money paid from the HH bonds is subject to taxation.

Money Market Accounts

Many financial planners suggest that an individual should have cash accounts equal to three to six months living expenses in case of an emergency such as may be caused by a health problem or employment termination. To the extent possible, this cash should be held so as to generate as high a rate of return as possible. In the late seventies and early eighties money market accounts paid as high as 15-16 percent and were a very desirable form of investment. However, money market accounts today offer a much lower rate of return and are not as attractive as they once were. They may barely beat passbook savings accounts as a place to stash short-term cash.

Investment Grade Corporate Bonds

Apart from utilities, probably only half a dozen companies have triple A ratings on corporate bonds. Consequently, we do not consider only triple A bonds here under our low-risk, low-return segment since there are other corporate bonds which are solid in terms of their risk feature and offer a good rate of return. We do not consider in this section the so called "corporate junk bonds" which do have a higher risk, but also a higher return associated with them.

Long-term corporate bonds, of course, carry the risk not only that something may happen to the ability of the company to repay the bond money, but also that interest rates could rise and drive the value of the bond downward. Zero coupon corporate bonds provide a compounding of interest at high rates and can be an attractive way to accumulate funds for college expenses or retirement. These bonds create a tax liability each year while no cash is distributed to assist in the payment of taxes. For this reason, they make good investments in accounts of children 14 or older who have their own separate tax rates.

Residential Real Estate

Your home should be considered as part of your investment portfolio. Unless you have purchased your home on a speculative basis — such as in an area that may be in transition — your house should be classified as a low risk, low return investment.

Our tax laws favor home ownership. Interest on your mortgage payment and real estate taxes are deductible if you itemize deductions on your tax return. Rent on an apartment is not deductible. You may never have to pay tax on the appreciation of your home as long as your gain doesn't exceed $250,000 ($500,00 if you are married). What more could you possibly ask for?

The only investment consideration you should give the purchase of a home is cash flow. Do not commit yourself to so large an investment that you can not enjoy it. In any event, if you do purchase a home, have the withholding on your federal income tax adjusted to reflect the fact that your taxes will be reduced because of the deductibility of the mortgage interest and related taxes. Because a home can always be sold and the proceeds invested elsewhere, you might want to consider the home and its appreciated value as an asset that will be available for your retirement. Of course, you will need to find some place to live, but with the children grown and out, you may find an ideal retirement home that is much less expensive than the home that you lived in through the growing up years.

If the value of your home net of mortgage represents a significant percentage of your net worth, you may want to consider refinancing during times of low interest to create additional dollars for investment diversification.

Single Premium Deferred Annuities

A single premium deferred annuity is a tax favored investment that allows the investor to set aside a large sum of money which will be credited with an interest rate that is variable over the life of the contract. Most annuities in 1998 offered interest rates that varied from five percent to seven percent for the first year with no guarantee of interest on the annuity after that period of time. The single premium deferred annuity provides that the interest earned on the principle sum will compound annually until such time as the money is withdrawn from the annuity. Most contracts permit the investor to withdraw without any surrender charges up to ten percent of the total value of the annuity. However, under the new tax rules, any withdrawals from an annuity are taxed first to the extent of income in the contract. Furthermore, loans and withdrawals may be subject to a ten percent penalty tax unless the annuity is held for a certain period of time or unless the individual investor has attained the age of at least 59 1/2 before withdrawing the money from the annuity.

The advantage of the single premium deferred annuity is that it does allow for the build up of interest on a tax deferred basis, and therefore permits the significant compounding of money within the annuity contract. From this standpoint, the crediting of interest on the basis where it can compound over a number of years is an important economic phenomena. For example, if you set aside $20,000 today and in twenty years took that money from an annuity contract that provided for an average of 10 percent return on your money, the total amount of money that you would receive would be in the neighborhood of $134,000. If, on the other hand, your rate of return over that same twenty year period had averaged twelve percent, your total amount of money would be in the neighborhood of $192,000 versus the $134,000.

If you buy an annuity contract, you may be disappointed in your investment returns in the long run. During periods of falling interest rates, the rate of return on annuities will drop to meet market conditions. However, during periods of rising interest rates, annuities are not obliged to keep pace — especially if a surrender charge is applicable to discourage surrender of the contract. Most annuities have a back end surrender charge which may not totally disappear until after the eighth year. Thus, it is more likely that the interest paid on the annuity you have purchased will decrease versus comparable investments rather than increase. However, this investment risk may well be overcome by the tax deferred nature of the investment.

Measuring Your Tolerance To Risk

Rate yourself on a scale of 1 to 10 on each of the following

1) the number of years until retirement (the greater the number of years, the higher the score)

2) future of current vocation: both stability and economic potential (the greater the potential, the higher the score)

3) at your current rate of savings, the number of years required to accumulate your current investment dollars (the more years, the lower the score)

4) estimated inheritances as a percentage of your current investment dollars (the higher the percentage, the higher the score)

5) your tolerance to risk (the higher your tolerance, the higher your score)

6) the quality of your high risk investments (the higher the quality, the higher your score)

Add your scores. The higher the score, the higher percentage you should have in moderate and high risk investments. However, even with a very high score, you probably should limit your high risk investments to not more than 50% of your investment portfolio. On the other hand, a low score indicates a need to stay primarily in conservative, low risk, low return investments.

CHAPTER 6
PATHWAY NO. FOUR
MODERATE RISK, MODERATE RETURN INVESTMENTS

The types of investments discussed in this chapter are very popular. Many people believe that the types of investments categorized as moderate risk, moderate return are safe, productive investments and are inclined to place practically all of their money in them. But to do so may create a higher risk than is necessary to achieve a substantial return.

One of the keys to financial success is to monitor moderate risk, moderate yield investments to determine whether they should stay in that category. One stock in a portfolio of stocks can do so well that its performance becomes disproportionately important to the performer of the portfolio. Reliance on one stock carries a much higher risk than reliance on a balanced portfolio of stocks. In such a case, it may be desirable to liquidate some of the rapidly appreciating stock to take advantage of the gain that has occurred and to spread the risk over other securities. Otherwise, the investor may be moving from a moderate-risk situation to a high-risk situation.

Investment Funds and Mutual Funds

There are a number of qualified investment advisors who will manage investments for a fee that may vary from .5% to 2% per year of the assets. In addition to this fee, the investor will need to pay a discount broker to execute transactions made by the investment advisor. Investment advisors typically will not accept less than some minimum amount to manage, such as $100,000. Some of them only accept investors with $500,000 or more to be managed. Many of these advisors have had extremely good track records. Because of this, many stockbrokers have specific investment advisors they recommend. The stockbroker will then execute the transactions advised by the investment advisor.

Mutual funds are similar to the professionally managed funds in that they provide for purchases of many different kinds of equities and bonds and thereby minimize an investor's risk. Most mutual funds have fared well in recent years, but again, the key thing is the selection of the mutual fund and not just the investment in any mutual fund. Some mutual funds provide for a substantial up front load (as high as 3%) while others have no front end loading. The loading is not a guarantee of a better performance.

Corporate Bonds

The purchase of high grade corporate bonds was discussed under the low-risk, low-return section. Corporate bonds that are the so-called "junk bonds" are often properly characterized as moderate-risk, moderate return. Do not be mislead by the name "junk bonds." A junk bond is simply a bond that carries a higher rate of return and along with it a higher risk.

One effect of calling high yield bonds "junk" bonds is to scare off many investors. Would an investor invest in a stock if it were called a "junk stock?" Probably not. Yet there are many publicly traded companies which have junk bonds for sale. Should the stock in a company that offers junk bonds be called "junk stock?"

Investor experience with high yield bonds has been good in diversified portfolios because the higher yield has more than offset the losses from defaults on payments of principal or interest.

However, this favorable experience has been with the "fallen angels" - bonds which were higher grade at the time they were issued and later fell in quality. There is a new kind of high yield bond, sometimes called "Chinese paper", which is of very low quality at the time it is initially sold to investors. These bonds often are issued in the course of some kind of corporate buy out, and some of these bonds are even zero coupon junk bonds. Nobody really knows how these bonds, deliberately made "junk" at the time of issuance, will work out. If we have high inflation they will probably work out well. If we have a recession, they could be a disaster.

Convertible Bonds

A convertible bond is a hybrid between a corporate bond and a corporate equity. A convertible bond allows an individual to secure a fixed rate of return while having the right to convert the bond into a fixed number of shares of stock. Convertible bonds go up in value as the value of the stock into which they are convertible goes up and their value comes down as the value of that stock comes down. Regardless of how much the stock declines, a convertible bond will not decline below the value it would have as a bond if it were not convertible at all. Thus, convertible bonds are not subject to the same degree of fluctuation as corporate stock and are generally a safer buy than corporate stock. Indeed, a portfolio of convertible bonds could be developed which would be best characterized as a low-risk, low-return investment. It also would be possible, however, to put together a portfolio of convertible bonds that would fall into the category of high-risk, high-return investments — the point being that not just the particular convertible bond, but the overall characteristics of a portfolio of them that determines the degree of risk and return involved.

International Funds

It used to be that so much of world action in equities was in the United States that it did not make sense to view investments on a global basis. For example, in 1970 almost two-thirds of all stock market capitalization was U.S.A. based. Since that time, this percentage has dropped (to under 40% in 1998) and has continued to decrease to the present day. Foreign stock markets have been growing and they have been growing fast.

If you have shied away from foreign funds because of your concern about fluctuations in the currency exchange rate, keep in mind that this risk creates an opportunity. You should begin your foreign investing with foreign pooled funds which will take care of administration, currency exchanges and withholding tax. Plus, these funds will provide you with the diversification you need inequity selection. The pooled funds themselves consist of three broad categories: global mutual funds that can invest anywhere in the world, mutual funds that invest exclusively outside of the U.S., and regionally targeted funds that invest in the equities of specific countries or regions. Global funds offer the best opportunities for broad diversification simply because of their geographical extent.

Real Estate

Real estate can be a very attractive investment. It is the crown prince of leverage and one of the few assets bankers will lend 80 or 90 percent of values. Real estate not only offers a chance of appreciation, but if the real estate is improved real estate, also offers tax advantages through depreciation. Depreciation is a wonderful phenomenon whereby the investor gets to deduct over a period of time the value of the structure placed on the real estate. The deduction is from income for tax purposes only and has nothing to do with the true value of the building. Real estate losses are generally deductible only against other real estate gains or other types of passive income gains.

The safest way to buy real estate is probably through the "hands on" approach which puts the investor in the driver's seat with regard to what happens to the real estate. The investor becomes directly responsible for controlling the key elements of his real estate investment which includes the following: (1) selection of tenants; (2) terms of rental agreements; (3) arrangement of and payment for repairs and capital improvements; (4) maximization of rental return; and (5) determination as to when to sell or refinance. The problem, of course, with the hands on approach is that it can require a significant amount of the investor's time which may be more valuably spent in doing other things.

If he uses the hands on approach, an investor can deduct up to

$25,000 of losses from ordinary income. However, this deduction is phased out for ordinary income between $100,000 and $150,000. The term of art that is used by our tax laws for what has been called here the hands on approach is "active participation". Typically, an investor must own at least 10% of the real estate and be very much involved in its operations to be actively participating. Any limited partnership interest is a passive interest and can not under any circumstances be considered an investment involving the active participation that is required for the deduction of up to $25,000 in losses from ordinary income to be allowed.

The opposite to the hands on approach is the syndicated real estate investment in which a limited partnership or a trust is formed to invest in real estate. This type of investment generally entails the payment of fees to the general partner who has set up the program, but it involves much less work on the part of the investor. Limited partnership real estate investments can be very attractive depending on the fee that the general partner is taking out of the project and on how large a share of the profit realized upon the sale of the real estate will go to the general partner.

Most real estate syndications in the past were established to create substantial tax benefits. Now, many of them are being created to produce taxable income which investors can use as an offset to their passive losses. Any limited partnership real estate investment should be reviewed by your attorney or tax accountant to see how it fits into your current tax picture. Moreover, if the partnership is defective, you may be deemed to have purchased an entity that will be taxed as a corporation and you may lose all of your tax benefits.

In reviewing any syndicated real estate investment you will want to check the following: (1) the true purchase price for the underlying property — not what the partnership may have paid to have purchased it from the general partner or from a related partner, (2) the fees that are to be paid up front, (3) the share the general partners take on the back-end of the project, (4) the security of the tenant or tenants for the property, (5) the tax benefits that are involved in the project, and (6) the likelihood that the project will be economically valuable for you aside from the tax benefits.

A real estate investment trust (REIT) is a program that provides an opportunity to invest in real estate and remain liquid. Most REITs issue publicly traded stock and an interest can be easily acquired or sold. REITs do not provide any depreciation since the ownership interest is as a shareholder of a corporation rather than as a partner in a partnership. Because many REITs went bankrupt in the 1970s, the new REITs are being less highly leveraged. Nevertheless, an investment in a REIT should be given the same careful consideration as an investment in a real estate limited partnership.

The key to any real estate investment is the purchase of property that will appreciate. In 1982, I purchased an interest in a condominium in Naples, Florida, with another attorney. The cost of our condo was $120,000 which included all of the furniture and fixtures. Unfortunately for us (this is something we could and should have determined upon investigation) the developer of our condominium project planned to add 200 additional units in the next four years — all of which sold for a price comparable to the price we paid for our unit. Thus, there was no opportunity for our unit to appreciate because additional new units were frequently placed on the market to meet the demand. In 1987, our condo was still worth $120,000. In the same project where we purchased our condominium there were a limited number of single family homes. If we had bought one of these homes in 1982 for $150,000, in 1987 that home would have been worth $450,000. Therefore, for an additional $30,000 we could have acquired an investment which would have tripled in value as opposed to our actual investment which made absolutely no movement at all in value. This is an extreme example, but it does show that not all real estate is created equally. Here were two real estate opportunities within 100 yards of each other — one of which appreciated by a factor of 300% and the other which appreciated by a factor of zero. A key deficiency for us in this investment opportunity was the work of our real estate agent. We could have been given more information about our purchase and could have been lead by a bright real estate agent to the purchase of a single family residence. We would have had a better investment and the real estate agent would have had a larger commission.

An experienced real estate investor has said to me, "Never

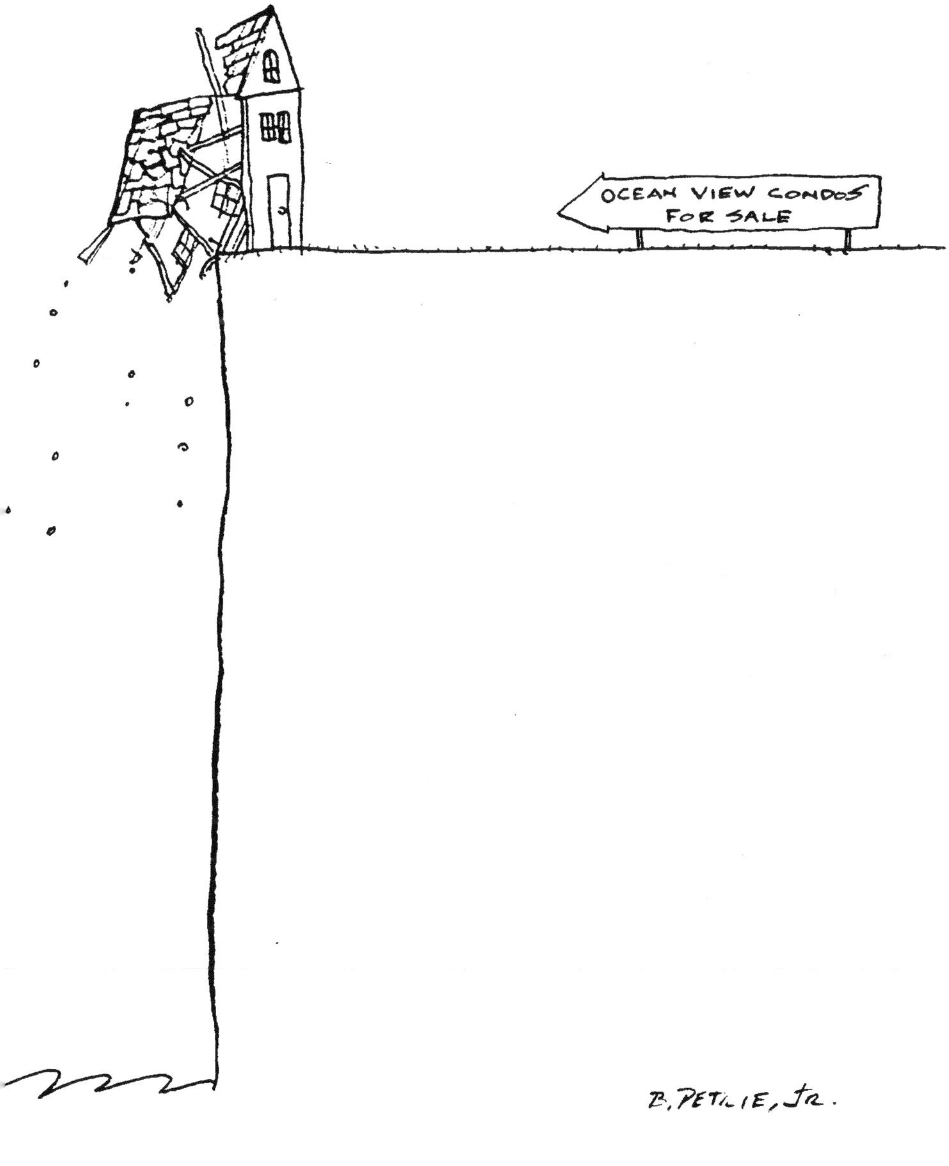
OCEAN VIEW CONDOS
FOR SALE
B. PETTIE, JR.

invest in real estate that is more than a 30 minute drive from where you live or work, unless you are buying as a limited partner." Although my Naples experience could have worked out in a productive way (if a single family residence had been purchased), it didn't. On the other hand, local real estate investments have been profitable for me. Thus, my experience tells me the real estate investor's advice is correct. What is your experience?

Closed-End Funds

Another type of moderate risk, moderate return investment that can have some real sizzle is the closed-end mutual fund. These funds trade at a discount (which can be quite large) and can create some very attractive investment opportunities. Many thanks to John Bowling, investment advisor, for this explanation.

The difficult part of describing closed-end funds is in the definitions. An investment company is a company that pools together the money of many investors to invest in securities. This means investment companies don't make any products; they just invest in the securities of other companies. There are two kinds of investment companies, and for better or worse they are called "open-end" and "closed-end." An open-end fund means it continually issues new shares when someone wants to buy them. These new shares are issued at price which is equal to the net asset value of a share for a "no-load" fund and at the net asset value of a share plus a sales charge for a "load" fund. An open-end fund also buys back its own shares from investors who wish to sell, at a price equal to the net asset value per share, sometimes, but not usually, less a charge. In contrast, a closed-end investment company does not continuously offer new shares to investors and does not ordinarily buy back its shares. It is just like IBM or other corporations; there are so many shares outstanding and you buy them from other investors, not the company.

Now we are going to discuss what enables you to make unusually good money out of closed-end funds. First, you should keep in mind that if you always buy things for less than they are worth, in the long run fortune will smile on your endeavors. This principle sounds like common sense, which it is. The problem is how do you know for sure that you are paying less than something is worth? With closed-end funds, this is not so difficult a matter.

Closed-end funds are bought and sold on the stock exchanges or over-the-counter just like other corporations and there is no particular reason why they should sell at their net asset value per share. In fact, they generally sell for less than that. Check *Barron's* magazine where it sometimes lists a whole flock of stock invested closed-end funds selling for 10% to 20% less than their net asset value per share. (When it does publish this information, *Barron's* is kind enough to publish the net asset value and prices and even calculates the discount or premium for you!)

The reason for discounts has never been fully explained, but mostly it seems to be a matter of neglect. Closed-end funds don't get much attention on Wall Street. The discounts fluctuate widely and without much rhyme or reason.

You do not have to be too shrewd to figure out that the closed-end funds at big discounts are better buys than mutual funds, for which you pay at least the net asset value.

The father of security analysis himself, the late Benjamin Grahm, discussed these bargains in his book *The Intelligent Investor*. After some analysis, Grahm wrote, "Thus we arrive at one of the few clearly evident rules for investors' choices. If you want to put money in investment funds, buy a group of closed-end shares at a discount of say, 10% to 15% of asset value, instead of paying a premium of about 9% above asset value for shares of an open-end company. Assuming that the future dividends and changes in asset values continue to be about the same for the two groups, you will thus obtain about one-fifth more for your money from the closed-end share."

The danger with closed end funds is that after you buy at a discount of 15% or so, the discount may get larger — say 20% or 25%. Any bargain may become yet a bigger bargain, but I don't think you can afford to refuse a bargain price because of that concern.

The key to making money in closed-end funds is a rather simple one. You buy an assortment of closed-end funds at large discounts. This by itself gives you a cross-section of the stock market at a discount and the discount would produce a mildly better than average performance if the closed-end funds you select have about average results. The next step is to simply hold what you have until the discount grows small on one of your closed-end funds. Then you sell it and buy another fund at a big discount. This process of regularly selling at small discounts and reinvesting at large discounts is a powerful money maker.

You may want to make a managed closed-end fund investment part of your investment portfolio.

CHAPTER 7
PATHWAY NO. FIVE
HIGH-RISK, HIGH-RETURN INVESTMENTS

For most people, the high-risk, high-return investment is the one which is most fun. It gives us an opportunity to be speculative, to put our money where our mouth is with regard to the future of some business, interest rates, energy prices, etc., and enables us to reap the reward of having taken a chance. If most people invested their money in the way that was the most exciting and interesting for them, they would invest their money in high-risk, high-return investments. However, because diversification is important for long term investment success, high-risk, high-return investments must be placed with other investments in a balanced portfolio. A sample portfolio is included at the end of this chapter as a model of a balanced and diversified investment approach.

A high-risk, high-return is any investment that has the possibility of an extraordinarily good rate of return. This is because the possibility of an extraordinarily good rate of return necessarily carries with it the opposite possibility and for that reason, risk follows the possible rate of return. If you can satisfy yourself that this is not the case with a particular investment, call me collect. If, on the other hand, you find an investment with a high risk but low rate of return, run from it.

Individual Stocks

Although the purchase of individual securities seems to be a radically different investment from venture capital endeavors or the purchase of equipment leases or oil and gas ventures, it belongs in the category of high-risk, high-return. Individual securities typically have much more price variation than the market does as a whole or as mutual funds do as a whole. Most people tend to think of the purchase of securities as being moderate-risk, moderate return, but again, this is true only in the case of a diversified securities portfolio and not simply on the basis of the purchase of one security.

What if you buy four or five different securities? This is probably still high risk, high return. True diversification in the equity area probably entails the ownership of at least 15 different stocks.

Options and Futures

One way to minimize the risk of the purchase of an equity is by selling a call option. The purchaser of the call option will be able to buy the stock that you own at a fixed price, which obviously can be of significant value to the purchaser if the stock goes up. If the stock does not go up, you can keep the cash that you have received from the sale of the call option and also keep the stock. This is a way of increasing the rate of return on a stock which does not appreciate significantly in value.

However, most options and futures entail high risk and are part of a zero sum game. A zero sum game is a game in which the total amount gained is exactly the same as the total lost. In a zero sum game, there are only losers — no one really can win in the long run, because for somebody to do well, somebody else has to do poorly. In addition, there are commissions which have to be paid on the whole process. Options trading probably makes sense only if an individual believes that he has found somebody or some system in options and futures that makes extraordinary sense and is willing to take a gamble that this chosen method of investment will net a positive return in the long run. In any event, options trading and purchases and sales of futures should at most be a very minor part of anyone's portfolio.

Venture Capital

Venture capital is probably the most intriguing type of investment that is available today. Venture capital is needed for many start-up operations as well as for operations that have chugged along for a number of years but now need additional money to expand rapidly. Venture capital can provide a tremendous rate of return if an investment is made in a company which then goes public. Apple Computer, for example, made millions for some venture capitalists when it went public.

When making a venture capital investment, you should be guided by a prospectus which will outline the nature of the investment you are making and what you can hope for in terms of the future of the company. Generally, you want to do business with a company which is at least sophisticated enough to put together a prospectus, and you do not want to invest in venture capital situations that simply involve giving money to somebody to pursue an idea. If you like the idea enough, however, you may want to invest with or without a prospectus. Also, it is possible to invest in venture capital funds that will make venture capital investments and do all the investigation that is required for such an investment. These venture capital funds are very attractive and many of them have done extremely well for the investors. Nevertheless, never put any money into venture capital that you cannot afford to lose — there are just too many instances where a company has not blossomed as hoped after venture capital was raised.

Equipment Leases

The purchase and lease of equipment is similar to the purchase and lease of real estate with the following differences:

(1) equipment (such as printing presses, computers, and cranes) is generally not an appreciating asset, and therefore the rental payments must be sufficient to cover the actual depreciation in the asset and the return you expect to make;

(2) an additional first year expense can be deducted up to the

purchase price of the equipment. This additional first year deduction is limited to $18,500 in 1998 and will incrementally increase to $25,000 by 2003 (or thereafter).

The purchase of equipment by a corporate owner who leases that equipment to the corporation can be advantageous. The owner retains control over the maintenance of the equipment and the rent that is charged. At the end of the initial lease term, the equipment can continue to be rented to the corporation. When the equipment is fully depreciated, the owner may want to give the equipment to children or to a trust for the benefit of the children so that the income from the equipment will be earned by and taxed to the children to build up an educational fund. The children in this situation should be age 14 or over to take advantage of this separate tax bracket. In this situation where there is control over the purchase of the equipment and the receipt of rentals, the equipment purchase may better be characterized as moderate-risk, moderate-return. The key here is the stability of the corporation which is obligated to make lease payments.

The purchase of equipment through a syndicated equipment partnership clearly falls within the category of high-risk, high-return. As a limited partner, the investor will be required to accept some personal liability on the borrowings by the partnership for the purchase of the equipment. This borrowing places the investor "at risk" and enables him to depreciate his share of the equipment purchase price. However, if the equipment becomes obsolete, the investor may be required to come up with some additional dollars. Moreover, many equipment leases provide for an initial term that expires prior to payment in full of the purchase price. For this reason, the equipment may have to be remarketed after the end of the initial lease term when the equipment may have depreciated significantly in value. There have been a number of computer equipment programs where technological advances made the computer obsolete at the end of the initial lease term.

The better types of syndicated equipment leases have a financially strong lessee committed for a fixed number of years. The lease payments from the lessee will pay for the "at risk" borrowings

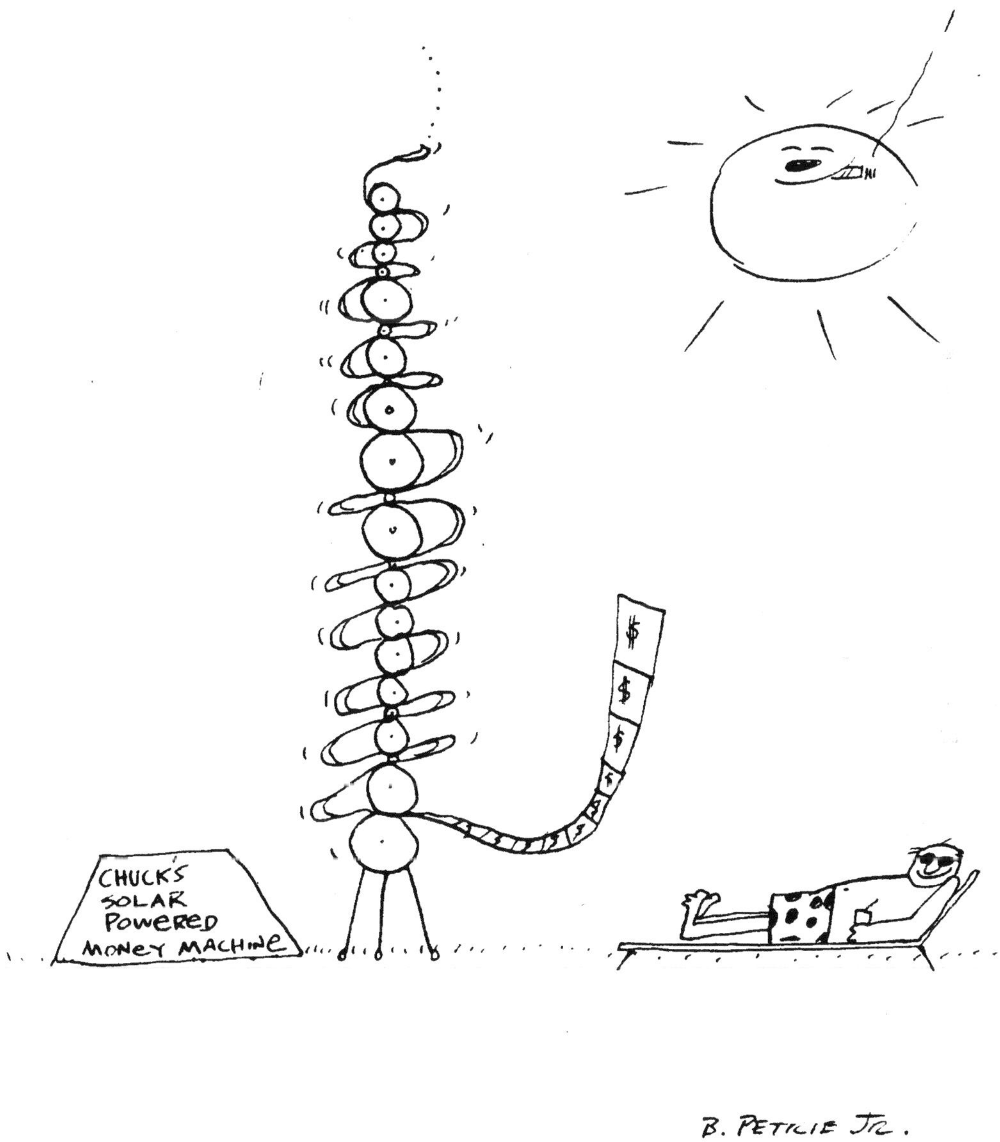
CHUCK'S
SOLAR
POWERED
MONEY MACHINE
B. PETRIE JR.

so the investor is protected with regard to his or her at risk commitment.

Oil and Gas Investments

With certain types of tax shelters, such as real estate or equipment leases, you can make some prediction about what the total economic effect will be. Also, you can get into each investment on a personal basis. The same is not true with an oil and gas lease investment. Here you are totally at the mercy of the general partners of the oil and gas venture to find productive drilling prospects. Because of the risk involved, you should be very circumspect in your oil and gas investments.

The tax advantages of an oil and gas investment are based on the fast write-off of your investment and the favorable tax treatment of income from a productive well. First, prepayments of drilling expenses in most cases can be written off in the year they are committed, whether or not actual drilling has commenced. Thus, for an investment of $75,000, the investor may be able to deduct a significant portion (such as $50,000) of that investment in the first year — even if the investment is made at the end of the investor's tax year. Certain expenses incurred in drilling operations are deductible, such as intangible drilling and development costs, in the year in which such expenditures are made. These expenses include the costs of the contract drilling and related expenses that have no salvage value (and thus are not capital expenditures), such as wages, supplies, and fuels. The ability to take these costs currently rather than capitalize them is available only to individuals who hold a working interest (as opposed to a royalty interest) in the property. Deductibility is limited to the amount of the investment dollars at risk.

If oil or gas is discovered, the income for tax purposes is reduced by the greater of the percentage depletion allowance, which for small producers is 15%of the income produced, or the taxpayer's share of amortized costs of the partnership properties. The small producer exemption limits the amount of domestic oil (one thousand barrels of average daily production) and gas (up to six million cubic feet of natural gas) that qualify for the percentage depletion. Also, a 22% depreciation rate is allowed for secondary and tertiary production. In any event, the important thing to remember is that any income that is generated by a productive well is subject to favorable income tax treatment.

There are several aspects of oil and gas investments that must be reviewed carefully.

(1) Are the general partners taking a risk, as you are in the investment? One item to look at in the prospectus to determine this is cost. If the general partner will pay ten percent of the costs (typical of many ventures where the general partners are at risk), you know the general partners will be at risk, especially if a high percentage of the money is going into the ground. Be very careful of turn-key contracts, where the general partner is agreeing to drill the well at a set price. The net price may be paying for the general partner's contribution to the partnership which may purchase a large back-end interest.

(2) How fertile is the region where the drilling will take place? Is the drilling "wildcat drilling," meaning high-risk drilling? Generally you should try to find a drilling project that is a combination of exploratory and development drilling.

(3) How many wells will be drilled? Generally the greater the number of wells, the greater the probability there will be a strike. Minimum for a typical syndicated oil and gas venture would be ten to fifteen wells. If you choose to invest on the basis where you are buying into one well, the advice here is to keep your interest small and to try to make many similar investments to spread your risks.

(4) If oil or gas is discovered, how much of the profits go to the general partners and how much go to limited partners?

(5) Are you buying a working interest or a royalty interest? Generally you do not want to have to capitalize all the drilling costs as you would have to do with a royalty interest.

With an oil and gas investment, your tax benefits are up front, and income tax consequences are incurred later. The liquidity of your investment is extremely low. Even in a very successful project, your after-tax rate of return will probably not be greater than twenty percent per year on your investment. The success of a drilling operation is generally reflected by the longevity of the income flow and not by what the first and second year return may be. Typically, it seems that oil wells produce much better in the initial period of time than they do over a long duration.

If a productive well or wells are drilled, you receive the benefits of the up front tax deductions plus the stream of income subject to favorable income taxes. If oil prices increase in the future, you can get a much higher rate of return on your investment than projected. However, the opposite is also true if oil prices continue their downward slide.

Oil and gas investments now are proving an interesting phenomena. When everybody else is running from oil and gas, it may economically be the best time for you to get involved. Why would this be true? When there are fewer dollars chasing oil and gas investments, the people who are making the decisions of where to drill wells generally have a better set of locations from which to choose and therefore can generally find better prospects. In addition, there are a number of drilling rigs which can be used on a less expensive basis because they are not in such high demand. Consequently, do not think that oil and gas investments are only desirable when everybody else is going after them.

In addition to what we have said with regard to what to look for in oil and gas prospectuses, the existence of any of the following should cause you to think twice about any oil and gas investment.

(1) A general partnership rather than a limited partnership. In this case, you have unlimited liability and if you are going to enter into such an investment, you should enter into it by having a corporation (for which you may choose to make an S corporation election) make the partnership investment.

(2) Lack of limitation on general and administrative overhead. Even if the general partner is at risk with you, he can recapture his risks through overhead charges.

(3) Conflict of interest on the part of the general partner, such as a) being able to drill for his own account; b) being able to farm drilling prospects from one partnership to another

(intra-program formats) — which is okay if an independent engineering firm is used to determine a fair term between programs; or c) being in the drilling business and having an opportunity to charge the partnership a noncompetitive price for drilling rigs.

(4) The drilling program will take place on a portion of a prospect (like a checkerboard) rather than over an entire area. In this case, profitable wells could be drilled on your partnership property and then surrounded by wells on property that your partnership does not own. You probably would not get a return in this situation justified by your risk.

(5) The general partner experienced a very large jump in program size, say from two million in the present year to twelve million the next year, and is attempting to raise twenty to twenty-five million in the year after that. It is too difficult to grow so large this fast.

Let's suppose your oil and gas investment is successful. Now the interesting time begins. To avoid income tax on your profits, you might consider transferring your interest to a trust for your children over age 13 or to them directly for educational purposes. If your investment return occurs in your retirement years, take the money and enjoy it. You might even consider rolling it over into another oil and gas investment if your income tax bracket justifies it. Because of the depletion allowance, you or your children will have to pay income tax only on some of the dollars received.

If your investment does not turn out to be the gangbusters winner that you hoped for, you might consider giving it to charity. In the early years, you may be able to show enough gas or oil flow to get a reasonable appraisal of your partnership interests and make more money by being charitable than you could by holding onto your investment.

If you are inclined to get into oil and gas investments, be certain that you get into bona fide programs and then diversify as much as possible. This "stick to it" attitude can pay tremendous dividends in the long run. If you spread your drilling risks out over many different drilling opportunities, you will maximize the opportunities for a consistent and good rate of return and improve your chances of coming out a winner in the long run.

Other Types of Aggressive Shelters

MOTION PICTURES

Motion picture investments offer a chance to make a quick profit if the film becomes an instant hit and offer substantial tax write offs if the film bombs. The beauty of the motion picture investment used to be that it could be speedily depreciated under the "income forecast method," which is based on the estimated box office life of the film. However, with the limit on passive loss deductions, you should only invest in a movie partnership if you 1) have passive gains to offset and 2) believe you will come out far ahead economically. Nevertheless, no one can predict the public acceptance of a film, even films with proven box office stars. Thus, the limited tax advantages, if you can use them, may only serve to soothe the pain of an investment that turns out to be nearly worthless.

AGRICULTURE

In the agricultural area, an investment in crops can result in a fifty percent to ninety percent first year loss, attributable to cost of labor, fertilizer and equipment. Risks include the weather and price fluctuations. The breeding of cattle can also generate very substantial first year losses, attributable to the purchase of an initial herd (and depreciation thereon) and grain costs. The sale of offspring will result in long-term capital gains if the livestock are held more than twelve months (twenty-four months in the case of horses and cattle). The risks here include disease and price fluctuation.

Intangibles—Precious Metals and Artwork

It is difficult to say to what extent gold should be a part of someone's investment portfolio. Some advisers feel that gold should comprise approximately ten percent of an investment portfolio because it is such a good hedge against both devaluation of the dollar as well as against inflation. We include gold and investment in other precious metals as part of a high-risk, high-return portfolio simply because of the uncertainty of the future of these investments. Gold can be purchased either through gold stocks such as International Investors or as tangible metal which can be locked in your safe deposit box.

A number of individuals have done extremely well with the purchase of artwork. People who are able to afford first class artwork for their homes, can both enrich the ambiance of their homes and make superb investments — if they are either lucky or well advised. Because artwork is subject to a subjective standard, it is very difficult to predict where any given piece of art is headed from a value standpoint. Therefore to the extent that an investor wants to buy artwork, he needs to consider the purchase of artwork a personal as well as an investment matter.

Re-Classifying Nature of Investment

It is very important in the financial planning process to monitor investments and to re-classify them as they have matured. Some investments that have become worthless should simply be written off to experience and not even be considered as part of your investment portfolio. Other investments that have done quite well should be moved from the high-risk, high-return over to the moderate-risk, moderate-return or even to the low-risk, low-return.

SAMPLE PORTFOLIO

Low Risk, Low Return

Investment	Percentage of Assets	Rationale
Triple Exempt Municipal Bonds with staggered maturity dates. Find guaranteed and non-callable.	15%	Safe investment with tax free return- staggered maturity dates give protection against rising interest rates. If interest rates are going up, can roll over bonds as they come due to higher return bonds.
Residential Real Estate	5%	Mortgage payments will increase equity over time and will give rise to deductible interest payment. Beats non-deductible rental payments. Obtain fixed rate mortgage while rates are low. Generally tax free gain upon sale.
Low Risk, Low Yield Convertible Corporate Bonds	10%	Provide interest return and participation in stock market. Bond characteristic decreases risk of declining stock values.

Moderate Risk, Moderate Return

Investment	Percentage of Assets	Rationale
Mutual Funds or Managed Investment Account - Portion in International Funds	15%	Diversified opportunity for investment growth. May want to have assets in an income stock fund as well as a growth stock fund. Monitor your return regularly. There can be vast differences in performance.
Real Estate - Individually Owned or Through a Limited Partnership	10%	Because real estate can be bought on a highly leveraged basis, growth potential is enormous. If we return to moderate inflation, real estate will appreciate rapidly in value.
High Yield Bond Fund	10%	This creates the highest income available and a mutual fund reduces the risk. If interest rates drop, this fund can spin off additional profit. During times of rising interest rates, consider shifting to money market accounts until you believe the rates have peaked.

High Risk, High Return

Investment	Percentage of Assets	Rationale
Individual Stocks - You Pick-em	10%	Gives you some experience in selecting stock - what do you look for in a company or whose advice do you follow? Also, can be both fun and profitable. Some people have an excellent sense in picking stocks - are you one of them?
Oil and Gas Ventures	10%	Working interests are still subject to favorable tax treatment and can shelter earned and other income. Even if not a working interest, income potential can be significant - especially since there is room for oil and gas prices to rise in the long run.

Investment	Percentage of Assets	Rationale
Venture Capital Funds	5%	Opportunity to profit from contributing to new business ventures. A fund takes some of the risk out of individual selection and enables you to spread your investment across many different companies.
Gold and Precious Metals	5%	Hedge against inflation, can provide some psychological comfort when it looks like everything else is going to the dogs.

This type of portfolio gives the investor balance with some protection if interest rates move lower or higher. From a tax planning standpoint, investments should be made so passive losses are offset by passive income. Depending on an investors previous investment history, this may mean shifting some assets to limited partnerships which produce a positive income tax flow.

CHAPTER 8
AVOIDING BAD INVESTMENTS

Investors can struggle with poor investments over a lifetime because they are subject to bad advice, second guessing, market rumors, bad luck, and misinformation. Nevertheless, there are common problems that all investors face that can be seductive in nature. Thus, it is very important that they be identified and factored into any investment decision.

The following is based on information learned over years of experience.

I. **Failure to Take Enough Risk.** Figure 8.1 shows to what extent investors do better in the stock market versus other investments over a long period of time. Unless someone is investing for the short term - such as for a college fund or whatever - it makes sense to have some significant monies in the stock market. The key is what is the total return on an investment, not just what is the income element. People who would invest just for income need to understand that the income produced by an investment consists of both cash produced plus appreciation. In many cases, people who invest for income would be much better off investing in the stock market and simply drawing out cash by cashing dividend checks and selling shares for whatever additional income they need.

Example: Michelle was a beneficiary of a $250,000 gift from her parents. She used part of the money as a down-payment on a new home and then wanted to invest the rest to produce high income to provide assistance with the home mortgage. Upon consulting an investment advisor, Michelle was informed that she should invest for the long term and simply pull out of her investment funds whatever money she needed for her current living situation. This way, she will

The Case For Long Term Investing
Year End 1925 = $1.00

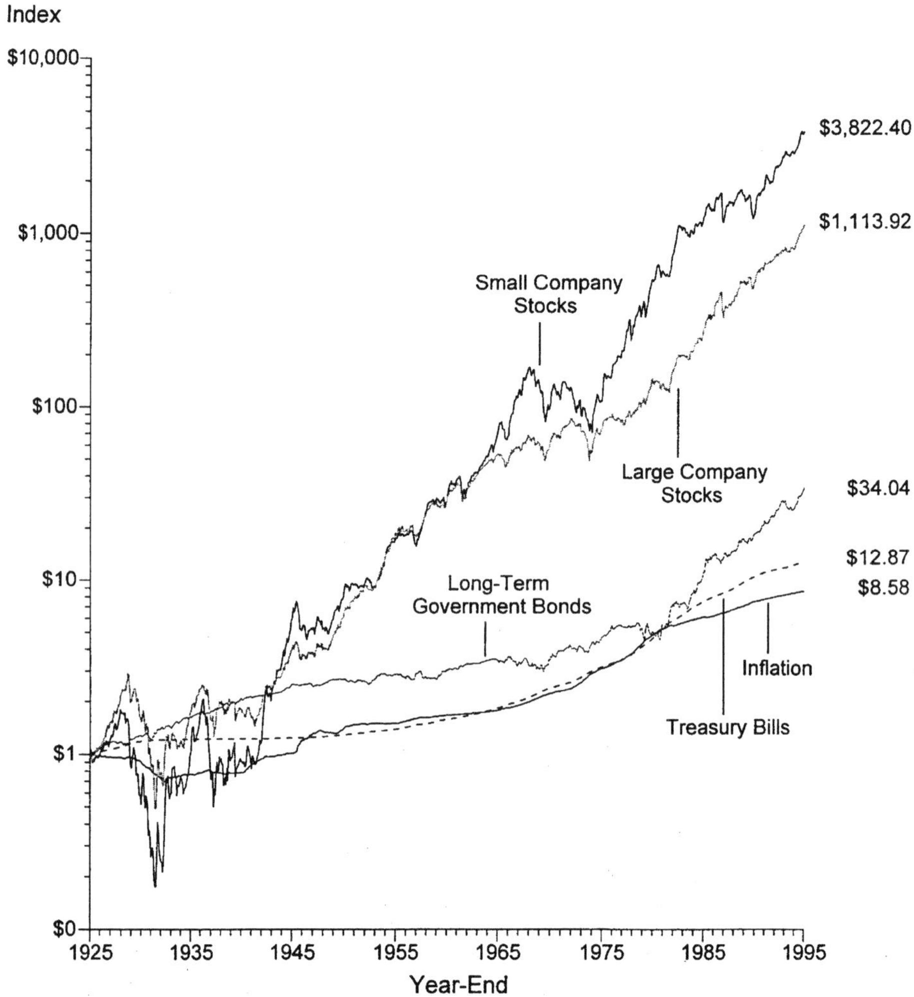

Figure 8.1

Source: Stocks, Bonds, Bills and Inflation: 1997 Yearbook, Chicago: Ibbotson Associates, 1997

maximize the total return over a long period of time by maintaining exposure to the equity markets.

II. **Attempting to Time the Market.** Market timers try to avoid bear markets when all the signs are there for a downturn. But in the process they may miss the very best opportunities for high yields through equity investments.

The following bar chart shows that investors receive very average returns in the stock market over a period of time if they miss the very best days of performance.

The Impact of Missing the "Best" Days in the Market (1982-1996)
(Annual Return Percentage)

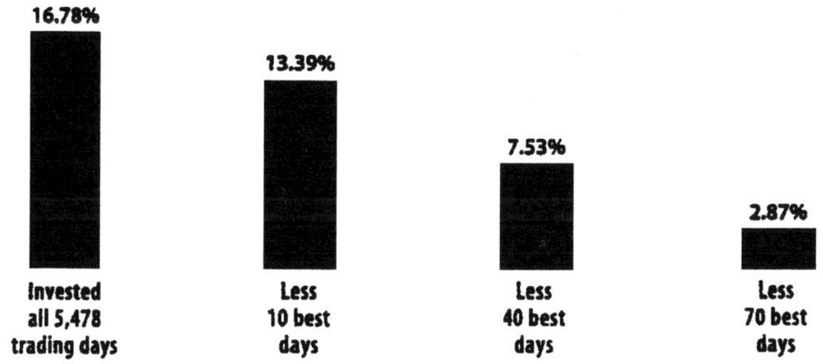

Based on the daily total returns of the S&P 500 Index. It assumes that all dividends were reinvested and that there were no investment fees, sales charges or taxes paid during the period. The returns shown above have been annualized. The chart is for illustrative purposes only and is not representative of any Goldman Sachs Fund. Past performance is not indicative of future results. Investors cannot invest in the Index directly.

(Goldman Sachs Capital Growth Fund, Annual Report)
(January 31, 1998)

This means that it can be risky to be out of the market just as it can be risky to be in it. The stock market has consistently rewarded patient investors who have made long term commitments to equity performance.

III. **Taking Too Much Risk.** A lot of investors like the idea of hitting a home run and will go overboard with investments that seem to be excellent investments. There are no guarantees and patience is a virtue. The fact that some investment has done very well in the past is not a predictor of what will happen in the future. Sometimes a wait and see approach is the best.

Example: Frank bought warrants of a pharmaceutical company that allowed him to purchase stock for $2 per share. When the stock climbed in value far in excess of Frank's option price, Frank chose to exercise the warrants early even though the stock was restricted and subject to a two year holding period. Before his two year holding period expired, the pharmaceutical company had some problems with the quality of its products and the stock fell precipitously. Frank was unable to recoup his investment. If Frank had waited to exercise his warrants, he would have avoided significant losses.

IV. **Failure to Diversify**. It can be extremely difficult to sell investments that have had a great run up. Yet, the rule is to keep any investment at a manageable level of one's portfolio and diversification is a must.

Example: Henry made a small fortune, at least on paper, by making an investment in a corporation before it went public. Because his investment appreciated by a factor of almost 20, Henry chose to sell only a small portion of his holdings to avoid a big tax bite. The corporation failed to develop new products and its stock price collapsed as profits plunged. Henry would have done much better if he had sold more of his initial investment and diversified in the stock of other companies.

V. **Misrepresentations.** Investors need to keep in mind that wherever there is an opportunity to buy, there is also someone who wants to sell. Be sure that you understand all of the facts of a situation and, if possible, bring in a third party to help review any major investment decisions that you make. The world is filled with individuals who will convey information that is neither complete nor factual and caveat emptor - buyer beware - applies to almost every investment decision that is made.

Example: David retired from a major publicly traded corporation with a substantial severance pay. In order to offset some of his income, he invested in a movie partnership as a limited partner. When he researched his investment a couple of years later to determine why he wasn't getting any return on his investment, he determined that the movie that had been allocated to him for resales through the video markets was not available and that it was unlikely he was ever going to see any return on his investment.

VI. **Pursuing the Latest Success.** It is tempting to jump on the bandwagon when things are going well. Yet investors need to be reminded of the fact that last week's success may be next week's failure.

Example: In 1987 Ralph was heavily invested in the bond markets through most of the year. In 1987 interest rates kept rising and rising which meant that the value of his bonds kept falling and falling. Ralph became increasingly distressed as he watched the stock market go up. In late summer 1987 Ralph made the switch from bonds to stocks thinking that the stock market was the place to be. Not only did Ralph participate in the 1987 crash of the stock market, but he missed out completely on the glorious rise of the bond market that occurred after the crash.

VII. **Failure to Check with an Independent Third Person.** Too often an individual makes the leap of faith without adequate information. With significant investments, an investor should spend the time and effort to hire somebody knowledgeable in investments to get a good independent viewpoint.

Example: Through his wife, Joe met a friend in southwestern Florida who was knowledgeable about real estate investments. Joe made a modest investment in a limited partnership and then talked to the Florida real estate man about doing something on a more private basis. Together they purchased a commercial building in Ft. Myers, Florida. It turned out that the Florida investor was unable to support the project from a cash flow standpoint and Joe had to foot all of the cash flow expenses and basically take over the investment. An independent third party may have alerted Joe to the substantial risk he was taking when he was the only financial backer for the project.

Not all of the above situations had to turn out the way they did. However, investors stand a much better chance of being successful with their investments if they proceed on an informed basis and watch out for some of these common pitfalls.

CHAPTER 9
PATHWAY NO. SIX
INCOME TAX PLANNING

I'm proud to be paying taxes in the United States. The only thing is — I could be just as proud paying for half the money.
Arthur Godfrey

For many individuals, income tax planning used to consist of little more than the purchase of high-risk tax shelters and the maximizing of qualified plan benefits. There may have been nothing seriously wrong with this strategy but the rules have changed dramatically since 1986. However, there are still some important opportunities to save on income taxes.

How to Shift the Income

For the most part, salaries and wages are not under your control unless you are self-employed. However, you can control the timing of income from other sources. The sale of stock or property and the receipt of a pension can be timed by you so it is received in a year when taxes can be saved.

One option that is readily available to you for the shifting of income is to transfer some of your money market assets to Treasury Bills that would mature next year. By doing this, you would defer the receipt of income on the cash invested until the T-Bills mature. Otherwise, you would be taxed this year on the interest earned from your money market investments.

Intra-Family Tax Planning

One of the key components of financial planning is providing for educational expenses. The cost of college is an enormous expense and one that grows more so each passing year. There are some ways to help provide for college expenses, even college expenses that are being incurred now, by enabling the taxpayer to take advantage of his children's lower tax brackets. Keep in mind that children under the age of 14 pay tax at the higher of their own tax rate or their parent's highest marginal rate on all unearned income over $1,000. Thus, there is little opportunity to do intra-family tax planning with younger children.

The techniques that we will discuss are the Minor's Trust and gift and lease back. In addition to this, the 1997 Taxpayer's Relief Act provides two new credits (the Hope Scholarship credit and the Lifetime Learning credit) to help you fund your child's education as well as the educational IRA.

The Minor's Trust

The Minor's Trust is a trust created for someone under the age of 21. Income does not have to be paid out annually as long as all the income and principal are distributed to the beneficiary upon attainment of age 21, unless the beneficiary elects to leave the money in trust. The first $1,700 of trust income is taxed at a 15% rate. Therefore, it is advantageous for the trust to retain at least that much income and distribute the rest to the beneficiary who will also be at the 15% rate (assuming the beneficiary is age 14 or over).

If it is desired to have a trust that will last past a beneficiary's attainment of age 21, the trust needs to be set up to distribute all income annually and to terminate at age 25. This may make sense where the parents do not want to create an opportunity for a child to get too much money at a young age.

Gift and Lease Back or Loan Back Agreements

An excellent way to transfer income to a lower tax bracket tax-payer is through something called a gift and lease back or loan back.

Again there are some very rigid requirements as to how this transaction must be structured to avoid IRS problems.

In this situation you transfer property either directly to an adult child or to a trust as a gift and then have the adult child or the trust lend or lease the property back to you. The net effect of this is to transfer income from you to the trust or to the adult child which will then cause that income to be taxed at a lower tax rate. You generate an interest or a lease deduction on your tax return and lower your overall income (and income tax) by transferring ownership of income producing properties.

This technique works best for the individual who has a closely held business and needs to purchase equipment for the business or who has an office building which he leases to his business. It can also work in the case of an individual who has invested in real estate that has become income tax positive. In the case of transfers of property that are covered by a mortgage, you need to consult with your tax attorney to make certain that the transfer will not be taxable to you. The problem with the transfer of property covered by mortgages is that a gift of such property is treated for tax purposes as though it were sold and you received a sales price equal to the amount of the mortgage that is assumed by the new owner. In order to minimize the risk of IRS challenge of deductibility of rent paid on the property transferred to a trust, it is very important that the transaction be set up properly. Tax Court decisions indicate the following guidelines should be followed in the case of transfers to a trust: 1) an experienced independent trustee, such as a corporate fiduciary should be used; 2) all documents should be executed properly, including the trust instrument, the deed, or bill of sale and a written lease; 3) the rent should be set at a fair market rate; and 4) the trust document must spell out the powers and duties of the trustee, including specifically the power to lease the property.

In making a gift and lease back of income property, two separate transactions are involved. First, you must make a completed gift. This means you must completely divest yourself of the property and deliver that property to the recipient. Second, you must have a lease executed which provides for fair rental to be paid for the property.

One federal court has indicated the gift and lease back or loan back transaction is valid only if there is a business purpose for the entire arrangement. However, the better line of thinking, which has been adopted by the majority of the federal circuit courts of appeal, is that the requirement of business purpose pertains only to the lease transaction, which must be considered by itself after the completed gift has been made. The Fifth Circuit, nevertheless, has attempted to combine the gift and lease back into one transaction and to impose the business purpose requirement on the combined transaction. While many tax practitioners think the Fifth Circuit's thinking is incorrect, you should pay attention to this approach is you live in the states of Florida, Georgia, Louisiana, Texas, Mississippi or Alabama, all of which still are or were formerly included in the Fifth Circuit.

Keep in mind that if you are making a gift to an adult child and then planning a lease back or a loan back of the property that has been given to the child, you must have confidence in this child's ability to deal with you on a fair and proper basis. Otherwise, you may find that the property that you have given has not been treated in the manner desired by you.

The Hope Scholarship Credit and Lifetime Learning Credit

The 1997 Taxpayer Relief Act provides two tax credits for educational expenses. The Hope Scholarship and the Lifetime Learning credit will both take affect in 1998. The Hope Scholarship gives you an up to $1,500 credit per student for such educational expenses as tuition and fees incurred during the first two years of post-secondary education. The credit is taken on the tax return of the person who pays the tuition. This may be the parent or even a grandparent. In many cases, it should be the child if the parents are in too high of a tax bracket.

The credit is phased out between $40,000 and $50,000 of adjusted gross income for single individuals and between $80,000 and $100,000 of adjusted gross income for a couple filing a joint return. The credit is calculated on 100% of the first $1,000 of tuition per year and 50% of the next $1,000 for a maximum of $1,500 per year. In order to get the full credit, at least $2,000 of tuition has to be paid.

The Lifetime Learning credit provides a maximum credit of $1,000 for tuition and fees paid after June 30, 1998. Starting in 2003, this maximum credit will be increased to $2,000. You can claim the Lifetime Learning credit for an unlimited number of years but you cannot claim both credits at the same time for the same child. As there are a number of other limitations and phase-outs for both credits, check with your tax advisor as to how you should utilize them.

These additions to the tax law are definitely helpful for families that qualify from an income level and should not be ignored in planning to come up with college money. In fact, in many families, it is one more reason for children to work to get income that will qualify them for these credits.

Deductible Interest on Educational Loans

The 1997 taxpayer Relief Act offers other ways of reducing the strain of financing higher education. One of these is the deduction of interest on loans for higher education. Starting in 1998, interest payments on loans for tuition and room and board expenses will be deductible up to a limit of $1,000. This maximum deduction will increase to $2,500. This is an "above-the-line" deduction, meaning that you can take the deduction whether you decide to itemize your other deductions or you choose to take the standard deduction. Be aware that there are phase-out and other limitation provisions with the deduction that may limit the amount you can deduct.

Educational IRAs and Educational Withdrawals From IRAs

Starting in 1998, you can take advantage of the tax-exempt status of an IRA to fund educational expenses. Subject to certain income limits, parents, grandparents, aunts and uncles, nephews, nieces, friends of the family - anyone who wants to help finance a child's education can set-up an education IRA for a child. Contributions to the IRA are not tax-deductible and are limited to $500 per year. The advantage is that when the money is withdrawn, the withdrawal is made on a tax-free basis to the extent the withdrawal does not exceed the amount of tuition that has to be paid. Money that is in the IRAthat is not spent on education must be paid out when the student reaches age 30 at which time the earnings will be subject to tax and a 10% penalty unless they meet some exception such as for the purchase of a home. The money may also be rolled over tax free on the death of the designated beneficiary to any member of the beneficiary's family who is less than 30 years old.

The income limits are phased out between $95,000 and $110,000 for singles and $150,000 and $160,000 for joint return filers. This means that if you are filing jointly and have income of over $160,000, you cannot establish an education IRAfor any child in your life.

If you don't qualify for an education IRA because of your income level, can you make gifts to friends with the understanding that they will then put the money into an education IRA? While this is probably going to happen, it is not a good idea. There should be a history of giving to people independent of the education IRA and there should never be a plan between taxpayers to obtain an improper result.

Usually a withdrawal from an IRA before you reach the age of 59 1/2 creates a penalty tax of 10% on the withdrawal unless you come within the reach of some limited exceptions. The 1997 Taxpayer Relief Act has added one more exception. Beginning in 1998, you can withdraw, penalty-free from your IRA before the age of 59 1/2 if the funds are used to pay for qualified higher education expenses. These expenses include tuition, room and board, books, fees, supplies etc. You will only have to pay regular income tax on the withdrawal.

One word of caution though, if the student withdraws money from an educational IRA, no Hope credit or Lifetime credit (described above) can be taken in the same year. This being the case, talk with you tax advisor about how you may best utilize your various options.

Other Options for Intra-Family Tax Planning

If you have your own business or are part of a company which is willing to help you in your tax planning, you should consider putting your son or daughter on the payroll in order to have income generated that will be taxed to them. If you own your own business, you can readily adjust your own salary to take account of the fact that you now have a son or daughter working for you who is going to require corporate money for salary expenses. If you are on someone else's payroll, you are going to have to show your employer that your son or daughter is worth every penny or else incur the wrath of your employer for adding a non-productive expense to the payroll.

Putting Payment for College In Perspective

Now that we have presented some of the better ideas for accumulating after-tax money for educational expenses, we need to add a word of caution. There is no indication that people who have higher education handed to them on a silver platter do better in life than people who have to work their way through college. Does it make sense for a family to impose severe spending restrictions on itself or even to go into debt to pay for a child's education? It may make more sense for the child to make these sacrifices since the child is the ultimate beneficiary of the education. By paying for a portion of the expense of what he or she is receiving, it is likely the child will understand better the value of a college education. Many families force themselves to save on an aggressive basis to pay for their children's college education. Yet, because of rising educational costs these families have to make even further extraordinary efforts as their children complete their college training. Doesn't it make sense for the child to contribute to the payment of the cost of his or her education?

One reasonable approach to paying for a college education is for the parents to pay for the tuition and books but have the children pay for everything else. Parents can require children to have their part of the money in advance before the parents will pay for the tuition and books. This approach gives the children the opportunity to do their own financial planning around college expenses and to figure out how they can earn the money to pay for a portion of their college expenses. If they can't come up with the money through work and save programs, there is always the possibility for them to find the money through some type of loan programs. The point here is that it does not make sense for the parents to make a huge sacrifice to send their children to college when the children are not making a comparable sacrifice. The college experience can be more rewarding if the children not only have had to make the grade to get in but also have had to make the grade financially to assist in the payment of those college expenses.

Management of Tax Oriented Investments

We have presented in earlier chapters a number of investment ideas that carry with them favorable tax characteristics and would like to talk a bit more about them here.

From a tax standpoint, the strongest investments are working interests in oil and gas ventures. These investments can provide deductions against earned income and also provide an opportunity for a significant return. However, they are a high risk, high return investment. Real estate is an investment with stronger economic characteristics and some modest tax benefits but does not provide for the same tax advantages as oil and gas. Most real estate investments are moderate risk, moderate return.

If you are looking primarily at doing something with low-risk, low-return investments to help out your tax situation, you might consider buying Treasury Bills that mature in one year at the beginning of a year and thereby shift the income from those dollars to a subsequent year. This, of course, is only advantageous if you are trying to shift income forward to future years, which right now seems to be a good idea.

Using an ESOP to Defer the Payment of Taxes

Capital gains tax on the sale of closely-held company stock to an employee stock ownership plan ("ESOP") can be deferred by purchasing stock in domestic corporations within a 15 month replacement period. The basis which the selling shareholder had in the stock sold to the ESOP will be transferred to the replacement securities and gain will be taxed at the time that he sells or disposes of the replacement securities.

In order to qualify for the deferral of the capital gains tax, the ESOP must own at least 30% of the stock of the company immediately after the transaction. It is not necessary that 30% of the stock be purchased from the selling shareholder. If an ESOP already owns 30%, any size sale can qualify for the special deferral. But, neither you nor a family member can be a participant in the ESOP which has purchased your stock. In addition, both the ESOP and the selling shareholder must meet a number of special requirements.

Planning for Divorce

The break-up of a marriage is tough enough emotionally without including the financial strain of dividing a couple's assets and after-tax cash flow. The tax law can be helpful in enabling a couple to split taxable income by making qualified alimony payments deductible to the payor spouse and taxable to the receiving spouse. In order for payments to qualify, the seven following requirements must be met:

1. Payments must be made in cash to or for the benefit of the receiving spouse;
2. Payments must be made pursuant to a divorce or separation agreement;
3. Where the spouses are legally separated, the spouses must not be members of the same household at the time the

payment is made;

4. Payments must not be designated as non-deductible by the payor spouse and non-taxable by the receiving spouse;
5. Payments must cease upon the death of the receiving spouse;
6. Payments must not be designated as child support; and
7. If payments under final judgments or decrees exceed $15,000, they may not provide for excessively large payments in the early years without running the risk of the early payments being subject to recapture in the third post-separation year. This provision is intended to spread out deductible alimony payments on a fairly even basis.

Deductible alimony can enable a couple dramatically to increase after-tax dollars available for savings or consumption. If spouse A, who is in the 31% tax bracket, is willing to pay spouse B, who is in the 15% tax bracket, $15,000 a year for alimony (and such payments qualify for alimony by meeting the above seven requirements), the couple will save $2,400 in net taxes.

Charitable Contributions

All of us will spend a significant amount of time and money in saving as many dollars as possible for income tax purposes; yet when it comes to making charitable contributions, we may simply write out checks to our favorite charities. This may be the sensible thing to do if those checks are small, but if we are giving significant amounts to charity, we need to follow some basic rules to maximize the benefit to us of our giving and perhaps even to enable us to give more to our favorite charities.

In general, it is desirable to give a charity appreciated property. The reason for this is that the taxpayer gets a full deduction for the fair market value of the donated property and does not have to pay any tax on the difference between what he paid and the appreciated value. There are some limitations on this, but those limitations apply only in the case of artwork and other tangible property and in the case of very large gifts — gifts that are in excess of thirty percent of your adjusted gross income. Also, the appreciated part of your gift now may trigger the alternative minimum tax; therefore check with your CPA before making a very large charitable gift.

If you own a closely held business, you might think of making gifts of shares of stock of your business to a charity and then, at some point in the future, having your corporation redeem those shares of stock. This is a way for you to use accumulated corporate profits in a positive way and costs you about $.33 on each $1 contributed to charities in 1998.

It is also possible to combine charitable giving with intra-family tax planning. For example, suppose that you gave appreciated securities with a value of $50,000 to a charitable remainder annuity trust (a trust which pays income to an individual beneficiary for a designated term, remainder to a charity) which paid nine percent of the $50,000 value for five years to your child who was about to head to college, and then at the end of the five years transferred the $50,000 to the charity. In this situation, the $4,500 of income per year would be taxed to your son or daughter at his or her tax rates (if age 14 or over) and you would get a tax deduction of approximately $32,000 for the gift to the charitable remainder annuity trust. Furthermore, you would not pay any tax on any appreciation of the securities that you gave to the trust.

Older taxpayers who may want to make certain that they have a good income flow from assets can use charitable remainder annuity trusts with themselves as the income beneficiaries. The trust can be set up so the taxpayer has a lifetime annuity from the trust and then at his death, the principal goes to the charity. This can be a very effective way to produce a high income flow, but at the same time obtain a large charitable deduction for a current gift.

Another technique which is the opposite of the charitable remainder annuity trust is the charitable lead trust. Here the taxpayer places property in a trust where the income for a number of years is to go to a charity and then at the end of that time the principal of the trust reverts back to the Grantor.

If you have items of art or of an educational nature, consider donating these to a charity that is specifically designed for such use, such as donating a painting to an art museum. The fair market value of the painting would be deductible against your taxable income. If you donate a specific object with a value in excess of $5,000 to a charity and the charity sells it within two years, the charity must report the sale to the IRS. This is to prevent an individual from claiming a large write-off for a donation that the charity sells for significantly less.

In making any gifts to charities, it is important that you keep records of the date, description of property, fair market value, original cost, and agreements as to use of the property and the amount you claim as a deduction. Be sure you give to a valid charity that has been set up for religious, scientific, literary, educational, or other charitable purposes.

Alternative Minimum Tax

The alternative minimum tax ("AMT") is a tax designed to impose on taxpayers a certain minimum level of taxation. The calculation of the AMT requires several steps. Step 1 - compute regular taxable income. Step 2 - add back tax preference items as listed below. Step 3 - subtract the exemption amount - the resulting amount equals the AMT base. Step 4 - multiply the AMT base by 26% - this equals the AMT. Step 5 - subtracting the regular tax leaves you with what the AMT will be.

This is a simplified procedure that does not consider every item that must be taken into account in making an exact calculation of AMT. The simplified procedure, however, will show whether you should have an exact calculation made.

The AMT exemption is also susceptible to a phase-out.

The phase out is as follows:

	Exemption	Phase-Out Begins	Phase-Out Ends
Married Filing Jointly and Surviving Spouse	$45,000	$150,000	$330,000
Single Head of Household	33,750	112,500	247,500
Married Filing Separately	22,500	75,000	165,000

The 1997 Taxpayer Relief Act does offer some minor reforms to the AMT. Starting in 1998, the exemption amount for a child under 14 who has unearned income is increased to the lesser of (1) $33,750 or (2) the sum of the child's earned income plus $5,000. The $5,000 is indexed for inflation after 1998.

A "tax preference" is an item that is treated differently for AMT purposes than it is for regular tax purposes. The most important tax preferences are as follows:

1. Depreciation
2. Long-term Contracts
3. Installment Sales
4. Tax Exempt Interest
5. Itemized Deductions
6. Tax Refunds
7. Personal Exemptions
8. Standard Deduction
9. Incentive Stock Options
10. Passive Losses

If you do not have much in the way of tax preference items, it is unlikely that you will have a problem with the alternative minimum tax. Nevertheless, if in doubt, it can be very helpful to seek further advice of a CPA so that some trial alternative minimum tax calculations can be made for you to assist with year end planning.

Capital Gains

The Taxpayer Relief Act of 1997 provides many new tax breaks for those who sell property at a gain. As this section gives only a brief overview of some of these opportunities, it is not meant to take the place of professional tax advice.

The first of these opportunities is that the top tax rate on long term capital gains of individuals, estates, and trusts is cut from 28% to 20%. Additionally, to the extent your gains do not put you above the 15% tax bracket, the capital gains rate will only be 10%. To be eligible for the rate cut, you must hold the property you are selling for more than 12 months before you sell it (this change to 12 months was made by the 1998 legislation).

This rate will be cut even lower for assets acquired after the year 2000 if the property was held for more than five years before the sale. If these conditions are met, the rate would be cut from 20% to 18% for those in the 20% income tax bracket and from 10% to 8% for those in the 15% income tax bracket.

The rate cut does not apply to the sale of real property (to the extent of depreciable deductions taken on the property) or collectibles such as stamps or coins. In regards to the Alternative Minimum Tax, gains taxed at a top rate of less than 28%, are taxed at the same rate for Alternative Minimum Tax purposes.

Sale of Principal Residence

Another important capital savings tax break is the universal exclusion for gain on each "qualified" sale of a principal residence. If you used the home as a principal residence for two or more years in the five years preceding the sale, you can exclude up to $250,000 ($500,000 for a joint account) of the gain from the sale. This exclusion can be repeatedly used on the sale of multiple residences as long as you do not use it more than once every two years. This replaces the over 55 one-time exclusion of $125,000 (although you may still choose to have the old rules apply under special circumstances).

The way the law defines how long you have "used" the home may be quite complicated and you may need to talk to a tax professional to see how the rules apply to you. That said, here are some things to note. If your spouse died before the sale or the residence was transferred to you by your spouse, the time you owned the property includes the time your spouse owned the property.

If you are in a nursing home, special rules will apply. If you owned the property at least one year during the five year period, and you become incapable of taking care of yourself because of illness or mental incapacity, and you continue to own property while you are in the nursing home, then the time in the nursing home count toward the two-out-of-five-year rule.

A partial tax break (calculated as a fraction of the exclusion limitation) is allowed for those who sell their principal residence before the two year requirement. The sale must be due to health reasons, a job change, or unforseen circumstances. The last of these reasons is yet to be defined by the law but most probably it will be of a seriousness equivalent to the other reasons that allow the partial tax break.

Small Business Concerns

The 1997 Taxpayer Relief Act provides a wide variety of tax breaks to those who run their own business. If you are in this category, you should definitely investigate how your tax position may benefit from the new law. This section will briefly detail a sampling of these opportunities.

The first major change to the tax law is that the Alternative Minimum Tax is repealed for small corporations. Usually the tax applies to corporations that have large depreciation deductions and loss carryforwards. This would result in the corporation paying more in taxes than if taxed by the normal rules. The new law exempts corporations from computing the Alternative Minimum Tax that had average gross receipts of no more than five million dollars during the last three tax years.

Another opportunity to take advantage of is that the law has expanded what is considered a home-office. Starting in 1999, you may take a home-office deduction for a location that deals solely with administration and management of the business. None of the services have to be done at that location to get the deduction as long as you do not have another fixed location that conducts administration and management.

A third tax break offered by the new law is that a construction loan acquired during lease negotiations will not be viewed as taxable income. This is allowed to the extent that the payment is actually used to renovate the property.

There are also improvements regarding retirement benefits in a family business. The restriction that all family members were regarded as one person thus limiting the amount that could be contributed to their retirement funds has been lifted. Now, each family member employee can contribute up to $30,000 per year to their retirement fund. Thus, more money can be contributed to retirement purposes than before.

Finally, you can get a larger deduction for computer contributions your C Corporation business makes to primary and secondary schools. Where in the past the deduction would only equal the basis of the equipment, now the deduction equals that figure plus half of the excess of the equipment's market value over cost basis. You can not, however, deduct more than two times depreciated cost in the equipment. The equipment must also be less than two years old.

Miscellaneous Tax Tips

1. **Consider Taking Out a Home Equity Loan.** If you have any personal debt such as car loans, credit card expenses or delinquent taxes, any interest charged on those debts is nondeductible. If you borrow on your home to pay off these debts, the interest on up to $100,000 of a home equity debt is tax deductible regardless of what you spend th money on.
2. **Combine Business and Vacation**. A deduction of up to $2,000 per individual per year is allowed for attending business conventions held on a cruise ship. In order to qualify, the ship must be registered in the United States and all ports of call must be located in the United States or its possessions.

   Even the cost of attending a convention outside of the United States is deductible if it is directly related to your business and it is as reasonable for the meeting to be held outside of the United States as in it.

3. **Purchase of Vacation Home.** If you use a vacation home as a second residence the mortgage interest payments on it are fully deductible as is the interest on up to a total of $100,000 of home equity borrowing. In order to qualify as a second residence you must pass a use test. You must use it for the greater of 14 days or for 10% of the number of days that you rent it out to others.

   Note, if you do rent a vacation home out to others for fewer than 15 days during the year, the rental income you receive is tax-free - you don't even have to report it on your tax return and you still get the full deduction for the mortgage interest and property tax deductions that are other wise allowable.

   If you do rent your home for more than 15 days, then the income you receive is taxable. However, in this case, you do get to deduct expenses related to your rental activity such as maintenance costs, insurance, advertisement and depreciation. But in this case you are limited to personal use of the house to less than the greater of 14 days during the year or 10% of the number of days that it is rented to others.

   If your home does not qualify as a second residence, then you may even get deductions for rental losses up to $25,000 provided your adjusted gross income is under $100,000.

4. **Putting Children on the Payroll.** Since children 14 and over pay taxes at their own rate, it can be beneficial to expose them to the work ethic. If you can find a place for them, put your children to work and pay them fairly for what they do.

5. **Use the Child Tax Credit.** As of 1998, you may claim a credit of $400 per "qualifying child" under the age of 17. In 1999, this credit will be increased to $500 per child. This credit is in addition to any earned income credit as well as your personal exemptions for dependant children. Remember, credits are worth more than deductions because you can write off directly against the tax with a credit.

Just make sure you have a "qualifying child" under the Code and watch out for a reduction of the credit for incomes greater than $110,000 for a joint return, $75,000 for unmarried individuals, and $55,000 for married individuals filing a separate return. For every $1,000 (or fraction there of) your modified adjusted income exceeds the preceding numbers, the credit will be reduced by $50.

6. **Self-Employed Health Insurance.** As of 1997, the current 40% portion of the cost of health insurance will be incrementally increased to 100% by 2007. There is a way to get that 100% deduction now. If you are self-employed, hire your spouse as an employee and have your business adopt an employee benefit plan that covers the medical expenses of all of its employees and their families. This tax break has been approved by the IRS and results in benefits that are fully deductible to the business and tax exempt to the recipients.
7. **Charge It!** Effective May 5, 1998, the IRS will be authorized to accept payment of taxes by any commercially acceptable means. These methods include charge cards, debit cards and (of course) credit cards. Depending on which cards you have and which cards the IRS chooses to accept, payment of your taxes in this manner may result in frequent flyer miles, free gas, cash back or other credit card benefits. Doing this will also help to improve your credit rating.

Disposition of Property

There are two tax savings opportunities pertaining to the disposition of property that can result in favorable tax benefits. They are the installment method of accounting, and tax-free exchange. The installment method of accounting is used any time a capital asset is sold and payment received in the year of sale is not 100 percent of the sales price. The non-taxable exchange method is utilized when property is exchanged for property of a like or similar nature.

Either of these methods may save taxes when you are selling property.

Taxable income from an installment sale is computed by multiplying the gross profit percentage by the amount received during the year. The gross profit percentage is computed as follows: a) subtract your adjusted basis (cost of property less depreciation) in the property from the sale price less any selling expenses to arrive at your gain on the sale; and b) divide this gain by the sales price less selling expenses. The resulting percentage becomes the gross profit percentage. This percentage is constant over the term of the pay back period. The amount received each year multiplied by your gross profit percentage is your taxable income for that year resulting from the installment sale. If the sale originally resulted in a long-term capital gain, then your taxable income will be subject to long-term capital gains treatment. The advantage of this method is to let you pay tax on the gain over the life of the installments, which may result in the income being taxed in a lower tax bracket than if it were all bunched in one year. However, you must be cautious with this method because even if tax rates will decrease in the following year, no one knows what will happen to our tax rates after that.

The non-taxable exchange can be an important planning vehicle. In a non-taxable exchange, no gain or loss is recognized when property held for productive use in a business or investment is exchanged only for property of "like kind" that will also be held for use in the trade or business. This can be of enormous benefit to a taxpayer who is "trading up" properties. It allows you an opportunity to dispose of your property, invest in new property, and not be taxed on the transaction. To qualify, there must be an exchange of like properties that were and will be used for business or investment. Your basis in the new property for resale or depreciation purposes will be the same as your basis in the old property increased for any additional cash you pay for the new property. Also, any "boot" (cash or property other than like kind) received in the exchange will result in recognition of gain equal to the amount of the boot received. It is not essential that property that is exchanged be of a similar or greater quality. Thus, apartment buildings can be

CHAPTER 10
PATHWAY NO. SEVEN RETIREMENT PLANING

If we look at the lives of 100 people born 65 years ago, statistically, one will be truly wealthy, four will have enough assets to provide for themselves, 35 will be dead and 60 will be dead broke. This is an alarming statistic. But no wonder. Over 55% of us believe that being able to retire with an adequate amount of money is a right as a USA citizen as opposed to a privilege (USA Today B-1, February 7, 1986). If retiring with enough money is a right as opposed to a privilege, some of us may ask, why save money?

Many of the same people who believe that retiring with enough money is a right will be dead broke by age 65. A financially comfortable retirement is not guaranteed by anyone. Social Security will provide only a portion of what you need at retirement. And if you work for a company that has a plan that provides retirement benefits, you may be shocked at how little money is available for you at age 65. Recent studies show an individual who has completed 30 years with one company and is making $15,000 per year will, on the average, receive retirement benefits from his company's plan of $385 per month. An individual who has completed 40 years and is making $40,000, will receive on the average $1,075 per month. This isn't much. It is the responsibility of each of us to act upon the law that savings are the cornerstone of wealth accumulation. When we plan our budgets, we should make the first item of expense a portion for savings. Why not pay ourselves to provide for our future before we pay others?

Calculation of Needed Retirement Income

One thing we have learned from the late 1970s and early 1980s is that inflation has a dramatic impact on how much money we need for normal living expenses. Although inflation is now at low levels, we must remember that some level of inflation will always be with us. Consequently, we need to build some type of projection for inflation into our retirement planning.

One of the most important steps in retirement planning is calculating how much retirement income you will need, taking into account inflation. Here's how:

(1) Calculate in today's dollars how much retirement income you would need if you were to retire today.

(a) Take your current after-tax dollar income and subtract temporary expenses (child support, education, savings, and other expenses you will not have at retirement). Gross up by 20% to allow for taxes. This will give you your minimum retirement income.

(2) Multiply this number by the inflation factor based on your years to retirement.

Years To			**Inflation Factor**		
Retirement	**2%**	**4%**	**6%**	**8%**	**10%**
5	1.104	1.217	1.338	1.469	1.611
10	1.219	1.480	1.791	2.158	2.594
15	1.346	1.816	2.396	3.172	4.177
20	1.486	2.209	3.206	4.661	6.727
25	1.641	2.687	4.291	6.848	10.834
30	1.811	3.270	5.742	10.062	17.449
35	2.000	3.978	7.684	14.784	28.101

Let's assume a four percent inflation factor for illustrative purposes. (If inflation is lower or higher than four percent, other assumptions used throughout, such as investment return on your money, will also change).

Suppose your present income is \$35,000 per year, your after-tax needs are \$12,500 per year (grossed up by 20% to allow for taxes to \$15,000 per year) and you would like to retire in 20 years. At four percent inflation, you will need \$33,135 (2.209 x \$15,000) per year of after-tax dollars to maintain your present standard of living at that time.

Where will all these dollars come from? If you refer to the part of this chapter that discusses Social Security, you will observe that if your present income is $35,000, you can expect to have 23 percent of that replaced by Social Security if the system is still around in basically the same form in 20 years. The same inflation factor, 2.209, must be applied to Social Security also, which means that we will assume Social Security will provide approximately $17,782 of the $33,135 you need (2.209 X .23 X $35,000). The remaining $15,353 of after-tax income must be provided through your company's retirement plan, your own IRA account, and your own after-tax savings.

The prospect of having to provide that much additional income each year when you are making only $35,000 per year can be mind boggling. However, it may not be as difficult as it seems. On a historical basis, you should be able to earn a rate of return on your investments equal to the inflation rate plus three percent. For an assumed inflation rate of four percent, your investment return should average about seven percent. This would mean that you should plan to accumulate savings and retirement monies that total about $219,328 in 20 years (obtained by dividing $15,353 by .07). You could then live off the investment return on your assets and save the principal to be used as a further aid in your retirement years.

Although the $219,328 amount looks large now, if you could invest $57,000 today at 7 percent compound interest based on the following table, in 20 years it would grow to more than $220,000 ($57,000 x 3.870).

Compound Interest

	5%	7%	9%	11%
5 Years	1.276	1.403	1.539	1.685
10 Years	1.629	1.967	2.367	2.839
15 Years	2.079	2.759	3.642	4.785
20 Years	2.653	3.870	5.604	8.062
25 Years	3.386	5.427	8.623	13.585
30 Years	4.662	7.612	13.268	22.892
35 Years	5.950	10.676	20.414	38.574

If you had started your planning 10 years ago, you probably could have saved at least that $57,000 today and would be well on your way to meeting your retirement objective — as long as Social Security continues in its present status. If you are inclined to assume the worst — that Social Security will not be available to you in any form when you are ready to retire — then today you need to have about $122,314 to secure your retirement needs in 20 years, all of the other assumptions remaining constant. Of course, one of these assumptions is that you can invest your money to earn after-tax interest of 7 percent or more.

This approach to calculating what retirement income you will need and what savings you need now to get there is provided as a worksheet at the end of this chapter. This brings us to the key to retirement planning and why it is so important for you to begin your savings program today.

Magic of Compound Interest

During the period of high inflation in the late 1970s and early 1980s, we experienced tremendous opportunities to invest and get extraordinarily high rates of return on money — such as 14 percent compounded interest. Now we are faced with lower interest rates, but with a strong stock market, we ought to be able to have a balanced portfolio that over a period of time will create a return of an average of at least 10 percent. Let's take a look at what happens to a $10,000 savings account over a period of 35 years based on an assumption of 10 percent.

Years of Investment of $10,000	Return At 10%
5	$ 16,110
10	25,940
15	41,770
20	67,270
25	108,340
30	174,490
35	281,010

It may take some searching to find investment opportunities that pay you after-tax 10 percent compounded interest for just one year. It is even more difficult, if not impossible, to find an investment opportunity which will guarantee an after-tax 10 percent compound interest for 35 years. Yet, in today's economy 10 percent is a rate many people expect to receive on long term investments. The more years you have until retirement, the more meaningful your present savings will be because of the magic of compound interest.

Tax Favored Savings

The key to retirement planning is savings. The key to what happens to our savings is the after-tax interest that we can earn on our savings. That is why retirement planning should involve investment opportunities that permit your money to accumulate on a tax deferred or tax free basis. The tax deferred or tax free return will enable more money to accumulate at a higher rate. If you own your own business, you have at your disposal the most powerful retirement planning vehicle available: the qualified plan. A qualified plan can be used in a very aggressive way. You need to employ an actuary or a tax attorney or some other retirement plan specialist to work with you to explain your options. Let's look at some of the tax favored investment opportunities available to you.

Single Premium Deferred Annuities

Although single premium deferred annuities were mentioned under the low-risk, low-return investment chapter, they should be mentioned in regard to retirement planning because they provide for the tax-deferred accumulation of money much like IRA accounts. The only difference is that the money that is placed in the single premium deferred annuity is not tax deductible whereas money placed into an IRA account may be. Single premium deferred annuities can be a significant part of an individual's retirement planning and should be considered in that regard.

Deferred annuities can offer investors a certain level of security from a downturn in the market and from creditors. Some annuities will also help protect you from bond losses and will offer benefits indexed to the performance of the market to lock in stock market gain. Some deferred annuity plans even offer a increased level of security should you find yourself injured or disabled. With safety, a deferred annuity can also offer you access to your money when you need it. Under some annuity plans, you can take your money out of the annuity without incurring any charges.

Deferred annuities can also help reduce the expenses associated with retirement planning. As mentioned above, interest income credited to an annuity is not taxable by either the Federal or State Governments until you take it out of the annuity. This interest income is tax sheltered and authorized by the Internal Revenue Code.

Even when you do take money out of the deferred annuity, the resulting rate is usually lower than the normal tax rate. Also, depending on what options you choose on the annuity, a significant amount of your monthly income may not be subject to income taxes. This results in more of your Social Security benefits coming to you. With some deferred annuity plans, many of the administrative, sales and/or investment fees are eliminated. Some even wipe out state premium taxes that you would normally pay.

In regard to increasing income, there are several options available with deferred annuities. Some plans offer the option of increasing after-tax income now or in the future and to maintain that level. This possible immediate increase in income can be enough to cover transfer costs of putting your assets into an annuity.

In a world of few guarantees, many deferred annuity plans can guarantee the amount and duration of your monthly income checks you receive. Deferred annuities can also guarantee that your principal will never be less than your original investment.

Finally, deferred annuities can give you more control in directing where your assets should go in the event of your death. Some deferred annuities with a properly identified beneficiary will bypass probate and eliminate all of the hassles associated with it (costs, fees, delays and publicity).

Tax Deductible IRA Contributions

Generally

Beginning in 1998, any person with earned income and a) not covered by a qualified plan and whose spouse is not covered by a qualified plan or b) whose earned income is less than $50,000 ($30,000 if single), can make an annual deductible contribution to an IRA of $2,000 or 100 percent of earnings, whichever is less (the $500 contributions to the new educational IRA will not count against this limit).

The earned income ceilings will be incrementally increased to $80,000 for joint returns by 2007 and $50,000 for single filers by 2005. If your income is over the earned income ceilings, there is a phase out of the deductible IRA contribution on a pro-rata basis. For example, a married individual with $55,000 of income in 1998 could contribute $1,000 to an IRA on a tax deductible basis. The phase out completely wipes out the contribution at $100,000 for joint returns in 2007 and $60,000 for single filers in 2005.

Contributions

You must be under age 70½ through the year in order to deduct your IRA contribution. Only cash can be contributed to an IRA If you have the cash available, you may want to contribute to an IRA as early in the year as possible to maximize the benefits to you of the tax deferred income.

Beginning in 1998, if one spouse is actively participating in an employer-sponsored plan and the other does not, the non-participating spouse may make deductible IRA contributions provided AGI on the joint return is $150,000 or less. There is also a phase out here beginning with AGI over $150,000 and completely wiping out the contribution at $160,000.

Even if you do not qualify for a deductible IRA contribution, you can still make a non-deductible regular IRA contribution of up to $2,000. Nevertheless, please be aware that the record keeping responsibilities that follow this choice are quite cumbersome if you want some future distributions to be tax free.

Withdrawals

Contributions to an IRA earn interest on a tax free basis. An IRA contribution of $2,000 per year will grow to $91,524 in 20 years, assuming an interest rate of just 8 percent. Unfortunately, the money can not be withdrawn without penalty from an IRAuntil you are at least 59½ and withdrawals must begin before 70½ (an important exception to this rule is withdrawal to finance educational expenses-see the previous chapter). The penalty on a premature distribution is 10 percent of what you receive. Plus you may be penalized on your investment rate of return for an early withdrawal and you will be taxed at the ordinary income rate on the amount you receive. Nevertheless, if you have a terrible income year and have a desperate need for IRA dollars, they are available to you. So do not think your IRA contribution is necessarily locked away until age 59½.

How to Contribute

The manner in which you invest your IRA is very important. IRA dollars should be considered as part of your total investment portfolio. IRA investments should be geared toward what will provide a high rate of return on a safe basis because you are not concerned about tax considerations in the type of return that you have. Life insurance companies, banks, savings and loans, and brokerage houses all offer IRA accounts. An IRA can not be used for the purchase of life insurance, since the money used for life insurance will not qualify as a deductible contribution. Moreover, you can not use your IRA account for collectibles, such as gold, art, stamps and jewels.

When NOT to Contribute

Is there any time you should not contribute to an IRA? Yes. Suppose you were putting in your last few years with the phone company before you start your own phone accessory business. In this case, accumulate every dollar you can for your new business. Also, if you have your own business and are thinking of establishing a retirement plan, you might want to wait until you have your own qualified plan. Qualified plan monies are more interesting to work with than IRA monies since you can be your own trustee and control investments. Moreover, you can borrow from a corporate qualified plan. Borrowing is not permissible from either an IRA account or from a self-employed retirement plan.

The Roth IRA

Congress has created a new IRA called the Roth IRA. In this financial vehicle, contributions to it are not tax deductible but withdrawals are tax free and earnings build up in the account tax free. Just like in regular IRAs, you can contribute up to $2,000 ($4,000 for married couples) per year. Contributions are permitted for individuals over 70 1/2. You can, tax free, withdraw an amount equal to your contributions whenever you wish. After five years, earnings on these contributions can similarly be taken out if you over 59 1/2, upon death or disability or to buy your first home.

You need to have an AGI under $150,000 on a joint return ($95,000 for a single filer) to contribute the maximum $2,000 (couples can invest up to $4,000). There is a phaseout after these limits where contributions are wiped out if your AGI reaches $160,000 and $110,000 for joint and single filers respectively. Until these points you can still make partial contributions.

You never have to make withdrawals out of this financial vehicle as you do in regular IRAs. Rather, if you do not need the money, you can leave the Roth IRA to your heirs and they can withdraw the money tax free.

Finally, although you can not roll your 401(k) plan of your company into a Roth IRA (as you would like to do if you are leaving your company), you can convert your normal IRAs into Roth IRAs. For more information on this, see the discussion on this topic later in this chapter.

Summary Chart of Phase Out Ranges

Because of the confusion that sometimes arises with what phaseout numbers apply to particular taxpayers, we have included the following chart that summarizes some of the phaseout ranges for 1998 returns.[1]

Adjusted Gross Income Phaseout Range ($'s)

Description	Joint Return	Single	Married Filing Separate
1998 Phaseouts:			
Education IRA	150,000-160,000	95,000-110,000	95,000-110,000
IRADeduction, individual with Pension coverage	50,000-60,000	30,000-40,000	0-10,000
IRADeduction, individual no pension coverage, and spouse having pension coverage	150,000-160,000	N/A	N/A
Roth IRA	150,000-160,000	95,000-110,000	0-15,000

1. Arthur Andersen, Small Business Services, FAX NEWS!, Volume 1, Issue 5, *Phaseout Table for 97 & 98* (Dec. 1997).

Defined Contribution and Defined Benefit Plans

Although we will not go into great detail about specific retirement plans in this chapter, it is important to review the basic retirement plans. A defined contribution plan bases contributions on a percentage of income (such as 10% of each participant's earned income), whereas a defined benefit plan bases contributions on what is needed to provide a fixed benefit at a stated age. As such a defined benefit plan bases contributions on income, years of service, and age. Defined contribution plans are more desirable for younger people who have many years until retirement whereas defined benefit plans typically benefit the older, more highly compensated employees to a greater extent. Defined benefit plans, depending on the age of the individual, can provide for contributions far in excess of those permitted for defined contribution plans.

Defined contribution plans and defined benefit plans can be designed to permit voluntary employee contributions. In the case of defined contribution plans, these contributions can be deductible if they are made to a 401(k) plan (also called a cash or deferred plan). Even if the contributions are not deductible, it is sometimes desirable that they be made since these contributions earn interest on a tax deferred basis and allow for significant accumulation of money. However, these non-deductible voluntary contributions now limit what other contributions can be made to a defined contribution plan. If you have some cash to invest and want to have it accumulate interest free on as rapid a basis as possible for retirement purposes, consider contributing money to your employer's qualified plan and building up interest on a tax deferred basis. However, this opportunity is only available to you to the extent your employer contributes less than the maximum allowable to your defined contribution plan (currently the lesser of $30,000 and 25% of compensation).

Defined Benefit Keogh Plan For Self-Employed Income

A defined benefit keogh plan can enable an individual who has self-employment income to shelter a very significant percentage of that income. Self-employed income includes money received as director's fees, commissions, teaching honorariums, and royalties. If an individual is employed by one company and has self-employment income, in most cases, he can set up a defined benefit keogh plan and shelter a very large amount of this money. Unless an individual has had a keogh plan in the past, or owns 50% or more of his employer, he can set up a retirement benefit under the keogh plan which can be based on a minimum benefit of $10,000 and can fund for that benefit even though he does not have $10,000 in income. Defined benefit keogh plans have been established for individuals who have had self-employed income from $4,000 to $12,000 and enabled these individuals to shelter the full amount of self-employed income. Because monies that have been contributed to any qualified plan accrue interest and other income on a tax deferred basis, a defined benefit keogh plan can assist in the rapid accumulation of wealth. Because of recent changes in the amount of permissible benefits under a defined benefit plan, only individuals age 45 and over will find defined benefit plans to offer much of an opportunity for savings.

Tax Sheltered Annuity

If you are employed by a non-profit or charitable organization such as a school, church or university, the best retirement planning vehicle for you is the tax sheltered annuity, often called a 403(b) account after the section of the Internal Revenue Code that authorizes it. In this type of plan, your employer may contribute to the plan for your benefit, or you may have to make the contribution out of your own salary, or a combination of both. The amount of contribution that you are permitted to make depends on your level of compensation and the size of contributions you have made in the past. The tax sheltered annuity program has the same advantages as an IRA: contributions are tax deductible and are permitted to accumulate income tax free. Yet it has the same disadvantages: you can not receive the benefit of these contributions, without penalty, until you have reached age 59½. More money can be contributed to tax sheltered annuities than to IRAs.

Excise Tax on Large Distributions - Repealed

There was an excise tax of 15% on distributions from qualified plans in excess of $150,000 per year. The 1997 Taxpayer Relief Act permanently repeals the penalty on excess retirement plan accumulations and excess retirement plan distributions. The law is retroactive to estates of decedents dying after December 31, 1996 and to distributions received after that date.

IRA Rollover

Suppose you receive a distribution from a qualified plan maintained by your employer upon termination of your employment after age 59½. You have two choices. You can pay a tax on the distribution (which may be at favorable tax rates if the distribution qualifies as a lump sum distribution and the favorable tax on a lump sum distribution is permitted) or you can roll over the distribution to an IRAaccount. The rollover to an IRAaccount must occur within sixty days of the distribution to you and enables you to defer tax on the distribution until you start receiving money from the IRA (which should happen after age 59½ and before 70½). Also, the IRA assets continue to grow on a tax free basis and can provide a very sizable sum for you at actual retirement.

When an IRA account is the recipient of qualified plan assets, it is called a "conduit IRA" This means that the assets rolled over to the IRA can be rolled out of the IRA to another corporate qualified plan. This gives you the advantage of maintaining control of these assets if you, for example, start up your own business. Banks, savings and loans, insurance companies and investment companies all have IRA account possibilities for you, including the conduit IRA

Before taking a large qualified plan distribution, consult your tax attorney or tax accountant to determine what is the most advantageous way to receive that distribution. In many cases, it makes much more sense to take the distribution and roll it over to an I.R.A than it does to pay a lump sum tax on it.

Unless individuals take some steps to protect their distribution, a lump sum distribution will be subject to a mandatory 20% withholding on all retirement payouts. The following should be considered to avoid withholding problems:

1. The plan participant must arrange for a direct trustee to trustee transfer of the lump sum distribution. This means that money being paid out of the company qualified plan must be automatically deposited into another qualified plan or an IRA. A delay even for a day will cause the 20% to be withheld.
2. You may permit your funds to stay in the plan (with the con-

sent of the plan administrator) and take periodic withdrawals or simply allow the funds to accumulate.

3. If you have already taken the lump sum distribution and found the 20% already taken out, you can still roll over the full amount by replenishing the 20% withholding with your own funds and then filing for a tax refund to recapture the 20% that has been withheld.

This law is a further example of the government infringing on the flexibility that employees have enjoyed in their qualified plans and IRA accounts. It causes some additional thinking before a distribution is to be received and cannot be ignored.

Roth IRA

There is also the option of rolling one of your existent IRAs to the Roth IRA described above. Starting in 1998, you can do this, whether you are single or married, in any year where your AGI is $100,000 or less. Income that is recognized in the rollover will not be counted toward the $100,000 limitation and there is no 10% early distribution penalty. If you make the switch in 1998, the amounts that are included in gross income can be spread ratably over a four-year period. If you decide to make the switch after 1998, you will owe the tax on this income all at once. The question then becomes whether you should take this action. There are pros and cons to the decision depending on the facts. As always, make sure to check with a tax expert that can help you apply the law to your particular facts.

Avoiding IRA Pitfalls

The following are some of the mistakes that people make with IRAs that should definitely be avoided:

1. **Borrowing from an IRA** - This is a prohibited transaction and can cause penalties as well as disqualification. The same holds true for using the IRAas a pledge for security for a loan.
2. **Investing in Collectibles** - This again is prohibited and any amounts invested in collectibles are considered as distribution. Collectibles include precious metals, art work,

and stamps.

3. **Taking Money Out Before Age 59½** - This usually would cause a 10% penalty unless the money is taken out over at least a five (5) year period. There are exceptions. You can make tax-free withdrawals if you take money out on a periodic basis, or are using the money for a qualified educational expense or first-time home purchase (up to $10,000). If you are interested in making withdrawals before age 59½, be certain to consult your tax adviser.
4. **Buying or Selling Property from an IRA** - This again is a prohibited transaction and can cause penalties as well as disqualification.
5. **Failure to Understand the Rules of Transfers for an IRA** - Unless an individual who inherits an IRA is a spouse, the beneficiary either has to take the money over a five (5) year period or over the individual's lifetime. The spouse of an IRA owner is permitted to rollover the IRA as discussed above.
6. **Not Making All Necessary Decisions by Your "Required Beginning Date"** - If you do not indicate how much you will withdraw after you turn 70 1/2 and over what period of time you must do it by this important date (the April 1 after you turn 70 1/2) these decisions will be made for you. This will probably result in payouts larger than necessary. This date is irrevocable so start planning a couple of years before this time so you can get comfortable with your decisions.
7. **Leaving your IRA to your estate** - Doing this will cause you to incur larger payouts during your lifetime as well as immediately ending your IRA when you die.

MISCELLANEOUS IRA TIPS

1. **Choose Your Heirs Carefully** - This decision can affect how much you are required to payout.
2. **Look Into the Possibility of a "Stretchout" IRA** - This lit tle known and understood option works best if you are sigle and you want all or part of your IRA to persons other than

your spouse. If set up properly, this option will some what lower you required payouts and (more importantly) allow what's left to continue on after you die. Thus, your heirs will benefit from decades of tax-deferred compounding on what remains in the IRA. Without having a stretchout IRA, the heirs end up having to take out all the money in just a few years and being subjected to up to an 80% taxation rate.

3. **Investigate All Distribution Options** - If your heir is a person or a trust benefitting a person, choose to make payouts using a "joint" lifespan as this will always lower your required payouts. In determining your lifespan, have the owner of the IRA use the recalculation method and the spouse use a fixed method. This is the best combination as you don't know for sure which spouse will outlive the other.
4. **Consider Making Charitable Bequests Through Your IRA -** Not only does the charity get the full amount of the bequest (since no income tax is due on the money), but you get the full estate tax deduction.

Non-Qualified Deferred Compensation

With the cutback made by prior law changes in the possible qualified plan contributions for many high income employees, the advantages of non-qualified deferred compensation plan should be considered. A non-qualified deferred compensation plan is simply an agreement between the employer and the employee whereby money will be paid to the employee upon retirement or to his family in the event of his death prior to retirement. Typically, a non-qualified deferred compensation plan utilizes the purchase of insurance by the employer as a hedge against the liability of the employer to make the payments to the employee. The funding for the program can come either from money that the employee defers from current pay or can come from other assets of the employer.

A more formal non-qualified deferred compensation arrangement makes use of an irrevocable trust which is used to hold the assets that have been set aside for the benefit of the employee. In a typical situation, three main legal documents are used:

1. An employment agreement which provides the basis on which the employee is to be paid;
2. A deferred compensation agreement which is an agreement between the employer and the employee whereby the employee is permitted to defer part of his pay that will then be set aside for him in an irrevocable trust; and
3. An irrevocable trust agreement between the employer and an independent trustee which provides for the assets to be held for the benefit of the employee. As part of the deferred compensation agreement, the employee would sign a deferral election to defer certain income from his pay, an election regarding how payouts would be made at retirement, and a designation of beneficiary form.

These documents must be drafted with some care because the intent is to enable the employee to receive a tax deduction for the amount of money that is deferred and then not receive income until the money is actually paid to him. To assure this, the trust must provide that it is for the benefit of the employee but that its assets can be reached by the general creditors of the employer. Typically, this is not a concern to the employee if he is dealing with an employer that he knows is on firm economic footing. The advantage of the irrevocable trust arrangement is that the employee knows that the money that he sets aside will be held for his benefit and that all of the money contributed to the trust plus earnings less taxes will be paid out at some point either during his lifetime or after his death. In addition, the employee can be certain that there will be no commingling of the assets of the trust with other assets of the employer and there can be no confusion about the benefit to which the employee is entitled.

The disadvantage of establishing a deferred compensation plan is that the money is taxed twice. It is taxed once at the corporate level when the money is deferred by the employee and it is taxed again to the employee when the money is distributed. The only advantage is that upon the distribution of the money, the corporation does get a tax deduction.

An ideal place for a non-qualified deferred compensation plan is in a tax exempt organization. In this setting, no income tax is paid so the deferral of the money works very much like a qualified plan. The only risk is that of the organization becoming insolvent and the assets of the deferred compensation plan being reached by the general creditors of the organization. The 1986 Tax Reform Act has limited the amounts that may be contributed to such plans established by tax exempt organizations.

Social Security

Social Security has been the whipping boy of the federal government for many years because (a) payments to recipients bear no correlation to what they have paid in; (b) payments to recipients bear no correlation to what their needs are; (c) the program is drastically underfunded; and (d) since a majority of today's work force is 40 or under, it places an unfair burden on the younger generation of workers in this country. Many believe this system will not, and perhaps should not, be around when people now 40 and under are ready to retire. Please see Appendix B for a proposal on what to do about our Social Security system.

Social Security was initially designed as supplemental income for retirees. Yet, it has grown to the point where many retired people are living entirely on Social Security. Thus, it has become a Catch 22 — we can not afford to live with it and many, many Americans can not afford to live without it.

Social Security replaces a much higher proportion of pay for lower income workers than for higher income workers. The following chart gives you some idea what you can expect to receive from Social Security based on your present yearly earnings.

Your Present Yearly Earnings	Estimated Percentage of Earnings Replaced
$20,000	48%
$30,000	43%
$40,000	36%
$50,000	31%
$62,700	25%

This table assumes you have been working regularly and that your earnings have been and will continue to increase with the average for the country. The chart also assumes that you are retiring at age 65.[1]

Since Social Security is substantially income tax free, it is a benefit you should not ignore. Yet, you may have to do some planning to receive it. One of the real tragedies of our system is that an individual is penalized for making money between the ages of 62 and 70. For these ages, every dollar of income earned above the Social Security limit reduces the Social Security the individual is eligible to receive. This means that our older Americans who choose to work are essentially subject to a tax of over 50 percent on their first dollars of income earned over the designated amount. Terrible! Furthermore, the Social Security income itself is subject to tax if the adjusted gross income exceeds prescribed limits. This tax can cause an effective tax rate of 25 percent of Social Security dollars that are received.

Receiving Social Security

A number of people who choose to work after becoming eligible to receive Social Security do not receive Social Security because their incomes are too high. There are some things that can be done, none of which are especially liked by the Social Security Administration. One idea is for the individual to incorporate, minimize his salary, maximize retirement plan contributions, and keep any residual income in the corporation for rainy days. This is a technique which the Social Security Administration may question but which enables the individual to accumulate additional retirement money for a later time.

In general, Social Security represents dollars that are free for the asking, and everything should be done to qualify for those dollars, short of giving up work. It is a shame that our system is set up to discourage people from working who may be at their most productive parts of their life. It is important that individuals who want to work make that rather than receiving Social Security their number one priority. Nevertheless, there are a number of things that can be done so that the individual can both work and receive Social Security and those need to be worked through with an individual's

1. See Social Security Administration, SSAPublication No. 05-10024, *Social Security: Understanding the Benefits* 35 (1997).

tax attorney or tax accountant.

Miscellaneous Retirement Tips

The Taxpayer Relief Act of 1997 will influence many aspects of your retirement planning. Here are a few of the immediate things that you should take notice of. Appreciation on assets held longer than 18 months will be taxed at a maximum of 20% so be sure to hold appreciating assets in taxable accounts. This maximum charge will decrease to 18% by the year 2006 if a five year holding period is satisfied.

You can also use home equity to help increase your retirement funds. The new law will allow you to escape tax on up to $500,000 worth of gains from the sale of your home if you are married ($250,000 if you are single). You can do this as often as you wish starting at any age. The only restriction is that you usually can not use it more than once every two years. Also, if you are married, make sure to use the exclusion while you are married as then you get the higher exclusion limit. If you become divorced or widowed when you try to use the exclusion, your limit will be cut in half.

With the repeal of the "success" tax, i.e. that tax that penalized you 15% on large withdrawals and bequests if you saved too much, now you should contribute as much money as you possibly can to your retirement accounts. Let the money stay there and build up for as long as you can. During retirement, use your Social Security, pension, and investment income before you use money in the tax deferred plans so you can accumulate interest.

Finally, in your retirement plan, don't overlook the increase in Medicare premiums the new law brings. The monthly Medicare premium in 2002 will be $67 or $804 per year. This is an increase from the old 2002 rate of $618 per year. The rate will steadily increase until it reaches $1,250 per year in 2007.

The best strategy in dealing with these increases is to plan ahead, before you become 65. Make sure to explore what other options you have besides Medicare such as Medicare HMO's and Preferred Provider Organizations. Each of these options offers different options as to the level of choice you have in physicians. There is also the alternative of a medical savings account. Contributions to such accounts are tax deductible and can be used for routine medical expenses.

Retirement Planning in Perspective

All financial planning will help to provide funds you can consume at retirement. Yet, if retirement planning is made a special segment of your planning, you can plan to save what you will need in a controlled manner and need not feel that you must accumulate an unlimited amount of wealth in order to enjoy retirement. When retirement planning is done properly, you can investigate investment opportunities and have some fun and success with here and now investments. Many fortunes would not have been made if people thought that the money that they were investing was for retirement purposes. Retirement planning needs to be placed in perspective. Not everything we do during our lives should be pointed to retirement, anymore than everything we do during our lives should be pointed toward any other single part of overall planning.

RETIREMENT CALCULATIONS

Years To			**Inflation Factor**		
Retirement	2%	4%	6%	8%	10%
5	1.104	1.217	1.338	1.469	1.611
10	1.219	1.480	1.791	2.158	2.594
15	1.346	1.816	2.396	3.172	4.177
20	1.486	2.209	3.206	4.661	6.727
25	1.641	2.687	4.291	6.848	10.834
30	1.811	3.270	5.742	10.062	17.449
35	2.000	3.978	7.684	14.784	28.101

Your Present Yearly Earnings	**Estimated Percentage of Earnings Replaced**
$20,000	48%
$30,000	43%
$40,000	36%
$50,000	31%
$62,700	25%

This table assumes you have been working regularly and that your earnings have been and will continue to increase with the average for the country. The chart also assumes that you are retiring at age 65.1

Compound Interest

	5%	7%	9%	11%
5 Years	1.276	1.403	1.539	1.685
10 Years	1.629	1.967	2.367	2.839
15 Years	2.079	2.759	3.642	4.785
20 Years	2.653	3.870	5.604	8.062
25 Years	3.386	5.427	8.623	13.585
30 Years	4.662	7.612	13.268	22.892
35 Years	5.950	10.676	20.414	38.574

FIGURE 9.1

RETIREMENT PLANNING

1) Take your current after-tax dollar income ________________

2) Subtract expenses and payments you will not have at retirement such as

home mortgage __________________
children's expenses _______________
savings ___________________________

Total Deductions _______________

Net is annual income needed if retirement were to occur now. Gross up by 20% to allow for taxes at retirement.

Net Annual Income ____________

3) Based on what you think the rate of inflation will be between now and when you retire, multiply the Net Annual Income calculated above by the inflation factor on the chart. This figure is the annual income you will need at retirement. (See Figure 9.1).

Annual income needed at retirement. ___________________

4) Calculate what portion of this income will be provided by Social Security. Multiply the percentage on the chart by your income and multiply this result by the same inflation factor used in 3) If your income is over $50,000 per year, multiply $8,400 times the inflation factor to calculate Social Security at retirement.

Social Security at retirement. _________________________

5) The difference between 3) and 4) is the annual income you will need from your own sources at retirement. Assume a rate of return on investments at retirement equal to the inflation rate you have chosen plus three percent. Divide this rate of return into the differ-

ence between 3) and 4) to arrive at the lump sum of cash you will need at retirement to produce the level of income you need.

Lump Sum Needed. ____________

6) How much cash do you need now to generate this lump sum at retirement? Assume a rate of return on your investment of the inflation rate you have chosen plus three percent. From the compound interest chart, divide the appropriate number into the Lump Sum Needed calculated in 5) to arrive at the amount of cash needed now to generate your retirement lump sum.

Cash Needed Now. ____________

If you do not have this cash now, calculate how much cash you will need in five years and start saving to generate this amount.

THIS ANALYSIS DOES NOT TAKE INTO ACCOUNT INFLATION AFTER RETIREMENT. HOWEVER, THIS CAN BE OFFSET BY THE FACT THAT WE HAVE NOT PROVIDED FOR THE LIQUIDATION OF THE PRINCIPAL SUM.

CHAPTER 11
PATHWAY NO. EIGHT
ESTATE PLANNING

Estate planning is a process. What is done today needs to be right for today, but also needs to be done with the realization that it generally can be easily changed.

Estate planning may be one of the most important things you will ever do. Since you have spent your lifetime building an estate for yourself and your family, you want to keep it with the people you love by paying the lowest amount of taxes possible. There are several techniques to accomplish this.

If you would like a quick overview of some estate planning ideas, please turn to the checklist at the end of this chapter. This will help you understand what, if anything you need to concentrate on.

Will

In most modest estate situations, the only documents that are needed are wills. A will is essentially a document which provides for the disposition of property. A will names an executor, who is the person who identifies and collects assets, pays off liabilities, and distributes the remaining assets according to the terms of the will. The will could also request the court to appoint a guardian for minor children who would be the guardians of both the persons and estates (any property owned by the children) of minor children.

A will should name a beneficiary or beneficiaries of the property and also provide for contingent beneficiaries. When a trust is used, the will typically will name the trust as the beneficiary of that part of the estate desired. When significant assets are owned, more is needed then just a simple will.

The Unified Credit

Estate taxes are calculated on the first dollar of each person's taxable estate. However, there is a credit against estate taxes, called the unified credit, which permits an individual to have a substantial taxable estate without having to pay any estate taxes.

The unified credit increased from 1982 through 1987 so that in 1987 and subsequent years an individual can have a $600,000 taxable estate without having to pay any estate taxes. This amount is known as the exemption equivalent. The 1997 Taxpayer Relief Act continues to increase this figure. Starting in 1998 the exemption equivalent will be $625,000 and will increase on a back loaded basis until it reaches $1,000,000 in 2006.

It is important that you and your spouse take the proper planning steps to minimize estate taxes if your combined estates approach or exceed the exemption equivalent. Otherwise, you could cause unnecessary estate taxes for your heirs if something were to happen to both of you in the near future. In an economy punctuated by a hot stock market, the value of your securities will appreciate markedly. Thus it is important for you to do the proper planning even if your present asset holdings are less than the present exemption equivalent.

The Unlimited Marital Deduction

One spouse can now pass an unlimited amount of property during his or her lifetime, or at death, to the surviving spouse without generating any estate or gift taxes on the transfer. The unlimited marital deduction creates the opportunity for a zero estate tax liability at the first death of you or your spouse. However, this technique must be combined with other estate-planning techniques in order for estate taxes to be minimized at the second death.

NOTE: If your estate plan consists of a marital deduction trust (see below) that was signed prior to September 13, 1981, your trust must be amended in order to qualify for the unlimited marital deduction. If the trust is not amended, your marital deduction will be limited to the greater of $250,000 or one-half of your adjusted gross estate.

Any property that passes outright to the surviving spouse qualifies for the marital deduction. Also, any property that provides income to the surviving spouse and over which the surviving spouse has a general power of appointment at death (the ability to direct whom the property will pass to) qualifies for the marital deduction.

A qualified terminable interest can also be used for the marital deduction as well. A terminable interest is a life estate or an income interest for lifetime in certain property. In order for a terminable interest to be qualified, the executor of the estate (or the donor if the transfer is made during his or her lifetime) must make an election to have the terminable interest property pass as part of the unlimited marital deduction.

The qualified terminable interest approach makes sense when one spouse wants to provide for the other but does not want to give that spouse unfettered control over the assets that comprise the terminable interest. For example, an individual with a $1,250,000 estate could make a gift during lifetime to his spouse of $625,000 in a terminable interest trust. Assuming he elects the marital deduction with respect to this gift, the $625,000 will not be included in his estate, even if his wife predeceases him. Also, the $625,000 can be used for the benefit of the husband if he survives his wife. In order for this to occur, the wife must elect to appoint an income interest back to her husband at her death. In this way the $625,000 can benefit the husband during his lifetime without being included in his estate. This type of planning only makes sense if (a) the donee spouse does not have substantial assets in his or her name; and (b) the donor spouse wants to exercise some control over the assets given to his or her spouse.

How Estate Splitting Works
(Based on an Equivalent of $625,000)

Suppose Frank has an estate of $775,000 and his wife, June, has an estate of $475,000. If Frank dies and leaves everything to June, there will be no federal estate taxes at his death. However, at June's death there will be a whopping $200,000 plus of estate tax that could have been avoided. And this calculation does not include appreciation of the assets left to June.

Suppose that in this case, Frank places as much property as is covered by the exemption equivalent ($625,000) in trust for the benefit of June and his children and leaves the remainder of his estate ($150,000) to June in a manner that will qualify for the marital deduction. A trust is simply a contract between Frank and another person, usually a bank, that requires the trustee to hold, invest and distribute property according to the directions Frank has given it in the written contract.

If the trust is written to restrict June's rights to govern the disposition of the property in the trust, the trust assets will not be included in her estate. However, the trust can provide for June and other family members to receive all the income generated by the trust assets and for June to receive additional trust property as she needs it. The trust can enable June to demand from the trustee each year the greater of $5,000 or 5 percent of the trust assets, without causing the remaining trust assets to be included in June's estate at her death.

At June's subsequent death, only the $150,000 that passed to her under Frank's marital deduction plus her own $475,000 will be subject to federal estate taxes. The remaining $625,000 in Frank's trust will pass outright to their children and will not be part of June's estate. The federal estate taxes on June's estate of $625,000 will be completely off-set by the unified credit.

The family trust can also provide for significant income tax savings. The trust can be designed to provide for a sprinkling of income among family members. Sprinkling means that income can be paid out to children according to their needs as determined by the trustee and taxed at their lower tax bracket if they are age 14 or older.

The money can be used by the children to pay for college, private school education, camp or any other expenditure their mother does not have a legal obligation to make.

The Marital Deduction Trust

In the previous example, Frank could have created the same favorable result by leaving his entire $775,000 estate to a trust that would have split up his estate into a marital share (here $150,000) and a family share (here $625,000). The marital share would be held in a trust - the marital trust - and the family share would be held in the family trust. The family share then would not be included in his wife's estate at her subsequent death.

The marital trust either must be a qualified terminable interest (discussed above) or it must otherwise qualify for the marital deduction by giving June at least an income interest coupled with a general power of appointment over the assets held in trust. The family trust, on the other hand, must restrict the rights June has in the assets held in that trust. The document that creates the marital trust and the family trust is commonly called the marital deduction trust. Typically the marital deduction trust provides for the funding of the family trust first to the extent of the exemption equivalent (the maximum extent possible without generating any net federal estate taxes) and for the remainder of the estate to pass into the marital trust.

If you and your spouse have combined assets that exceed the exemption equivalent ($625,000), you should each consider a marital deduction trust to minimize estate taxes at the second of your deaths. The larger your combined estates, the more important the adoption of a marital deduction trust becomes.

Selection of a Trustee

Typically, the spouse and perhaps a commercial bank with a large trust department are named as co-trustees of any marital deduction trust that will have significant investment property. The spouse is then given the right to dismiss the corporate trustee and hire a new corporate trustee if he or she is not satisfied with the initial co-trustee.

If your trust is drafted to provide that principal can be distributed from the family trust only in compliance with identifiable standards, such as that distributions of principal may be made only if necessary for the health, support, maintenance or education of beneficiaries, it is possible to make your spouse the sole trustee of the trust. In such a situation, you will still avoid inclusion of the family trust assets in your spouse's estate. Check with your attorney to determine if your family trust is drafted in a way that permits your spouse to be sole trustee with no adverse tax consequences.

Because a bank can be hired as an agent to assist in the administration of trust property, you may not lose much if your spouse is the sole trustee of your marital deduction trust. A bank or trust company can then be used to help administer only the property or assets with which your spouse needs help. The financial experience of your spouse plus the complexity of your estate are factors to take into account in making this decision.

Consider also making an adult child a co-trustee. A competent adult child could lend a valuable hand in decision making plus be available to serve as trustee in the event the spouse became incapacitated.

Other Reasons to Have a Trust

Even if estate taxes are not a problem for you, there are still important reasons you may want to have a trust.

(1) When minor children are involved:

(a) A trust that takes effect at your death can enable your spouse to save income taxes by paying income to or for the benefit of the children. The trust must be a sprinkling trust that we have discussed above to create the favorable income tax results.

(b) If a trust is not established, the assets that you leave to or for the benefit of your minor children will be managed by the person who is the guardian of your children. This can create a conflict and there is no way then of adequately overseeing what the guardian is doing with that money. You should have great confidence in the guardian if you are not going to have a trust because the probate court which will have some responsibility for monitoring what the guardian does is not going to provide the types of safeguards that an independent trustee would provide.

(2) A trust can provide an investment vehicle for your assets, and the trustee can assist your spouse in her financial planning.

(3) If you leave everything outright to your spouse, he or she may remarry and assets you thought would pass on to your children or to other family members may be transferred to someone else's family instead. This is not an uncommon circumstance and needs to be considered.

(4) The assets in the trust can be protected from the reach of creditors.

When to Pay Estate Taxes on the First Death

In many cases, it is good planning to provide for zero estate taxes to be paid at the death of the first spouse. The reason for this is that the surviving spouse can make gifts of $10,000 per year on a tax free basis to family members and thus minimize the size of his or her estate. There are, however, some situations in which estate taxes should be paid at the first death. Suppose you and your spouse are elderly and in poor health. In such a situation, it may make sense for some estate taxes to be paid at the first death to eliminate the problem of "estate tax bracket creep". Our estate taxes are based on a progressive tax system. If property is taxed at the second death that could have been taxed at the first death, it will be taxed at a higher rate if the second taxable estate is larger than the first. The concept of having some estate taxes paid at the first death is especially helpful for individuals who have combined estates of $3,000,000 or more.

Gifts Between the Spouses

In order to make the marital deduction trust discussed above work, it is often necessary to provide that there be significant assets in the estate of both spouses. Suppose John has an estate of $1,200,000 and his wife, Mary, has an estate of $125,000. If Mary predeceases John, then John will still have an estate of $1,200,000 with no surviving spouse to use for the unlimited marital deduction and for a marital deduction trust. In this case, John should make a gift to Mary of at least $500,000 so that if she predeceases him, she will have $625,000 to leave for his benefit in trust that will not then be included in his estate.

Planning for Individual Retirement Accounts

I.R.A. accounts are becoming an increasingly important part of estate taxation. In the modest sized estate, an I.R.A. can simply be left to the surviving spouse and the surviving spouse can receive payments from the I.R.A. over his or her lifetime. In large estate situations where the taxpayers are trying to take advantage of the marital deduction trust, it makes sense for the husband and wife to elect to have a large I.R.A. distributed over their joint lifetimes and to name the marital deduction trust as the beneficiary of the I.R.A. In this way, the I.R.A. will be paid into the marital deduction trust over a specific number of years upon the death of the owner of the I.R.A. The income from the I.R.A. can then either be passed through to the surviving spouse and taxed at her tax rate or some of it can be left in the trust and taxed to the trust at its rate. In this way, the trust can build up significant assets so that when the I.R.A. has exhausted all of its assets, there still will be assets left in the trust for the benefit of the surviving spouse.

Illustration: Joe has assets of $800,000, of which

$500,000 are in an I.R.A. account that consists of a rollover of pension plan monies from his former employer. His wife, Betsy, has assets of $200,000. Joe makes a gift to Betsy of $300,000, keeping just the I.R.A. assets in his name, and makes a marital deduction trust the beneficiary of his I.R.A. account. He elects to have the I.R.A. paid over his and his wife's joint life expectancy. This election provides for minimum payments but larger amounts can be withdrawn if desired. Also, the election can be changed every year up until Joe's attainment of age 70½. This planning enables Joe and Betsy to each utilize their exemption equivalent while minimizing adverse tax results from the payout of the IRA at Joe's death.

This program enables Joe and Betsy to minimize federal estate taxes and maximize the benefits from the I.R.A. account.

Roth IRA

If possible (your income must be less than $100,000 during the calendar year), consider converting a regular IRA to a Roth IRA. The portion you pay in taxes on the conversion will be out of your estate and the Roth IRA will be income tax free (but not estate tax free) to you and your heirs. This should result in comparable after-tax returns from your IRA assuming you will not be in a significantly lower tax bracket in the future. For example, if we ever do go to a flat tax system, tax rates will be lower and the conversion to a Roth IRA will probably be a mistake.

Private Annuity

In large estate situations, the use of a private annuity can be of significant importance. The private annuity is a sale of property from one person to another in which the purchase price is an unsecured promise of the purchaser to make periodic payments to the seller for the lifetime of the seller. Since the payments terminate at the death of the seller, there is no residual value in the estate of the seller.

Suppose that Marie, age 70, has assets worth approximately $3,000,000. She is unmarried and has one son, age 40. If she were to die without doing any estate planning, she would have a federal estate tax liability of approximately $1,100,000. As part of her planning, she could sell some portion of her assets to her son under a private annuity sale. Suppose she sells him $1,000,000 of assets. Part of the income she would receive would be interest, part would be capital gains, and part would be a return of basis. The son would get no deduction for the money paid to her and would not have his final tax results calculated until the death of his mother. If the son took the $1,000,000 of assets that he bought from his mother and sold them, he would be taxed at current tax rates on the difference between his total purchase price and the sale proceeds. This difference should be small if the son buys at fair market value, which he should do unless a gift is intended to be part of the transaction. If his mother died before all payments were made, however, the son immediately would be taxed on the amount by which the sale proceeds exceeded the payments actually made plus any amount of gain on which tax already had been paid. This result means that care must be exercised in selling property purchased with a private annuity, but it is not really a bad result. The private annuity in our example will have caused $1,000,000 in assets, less whatever payments are made, to be taxed at 20% long term capital gains rates rather than at 50-55% estate tax rates. See Appendix C for the value of an annuity of $1 per year based on different ages.

The private annuity can also be used in the purchase of a business between family members. The private annuity can even be used as a payment for removing property from the parent's estate, creating income for the parent, and generating payments that the child will more likely be able to afford than the payments that would be necessary to buy the whole business.

Planning for the Ownership of Life Insurance

Any life insurance that is payable to or for the benefit of your estate or in which you have an incident of ownership will be taxed as part of your estate. An incident of ownership entitles you to do, among other things, any of the following:

(1) To assign ownership of the policy;
(2) To change beneficiary;
(3) To obtain a policy loan;
(4) To pledge the policy for a loan; and
(5) To surrender or cancel the policy.

In order to keep life insurance out of your estate, you must give up all incidents of ownership in the policy. Also, you must live for at least three years after transferring ownership of a life insurance policy. In order for it to be excluded from the estate, the rigid three year requirement for the gift of a policy is independent of the value of the policy you transfer. If the ownership of life insurance will not cause any additional estate taxes, then it makes sense for you to own the policy and to control the designation of beneficiary and the settlement options. In this case, you should determine whether or not a marital deduction trust is necessary to minimize federal estate taxes at the second death. If the ownership of life insurance will cause or add to a federal estate tax problem at the second death of husband and wife, the life insurance should be owned in a trust that contains certain special provisions (a so-called "Super Trust" because it is so wonderful). When the insurance is owned in a Super Trust, it can be kept out of your estate and your spouse's estate, as long as you live for at least three years after making the transfer of insurance to the trust. If the insurance is purchased initially by the trustee and he has some discretion as to whether or not he had to purchase that insurance, it is possible that the three year rule will not apply.

The Super Trust must be irrevocable — this means you can not amend or revoke it once established. Also, the trust must be designed so that you have no incidents of ownership in the policy, and neither you nor your spouse should be trustee of the trust. You should consider other provisions to make the trust truly "super". (1)

Income of the trust will be used to pay premiums on your life insurance. This will cause income (and losses) to be taxed to you. If the trust borrows from a policy's cash value to pay premiums and our tax laws permit the deduction of interest on policy borrowings, that interest deduction will pass through to you as the grantor of the trust. As of now, no such deduction is allowed. (2) Contributions to the trust will be subject to withdrawal by your named beneficiaries. Inclusion of this provision in your trust makes it a "Crummey" trust. Crummey provisions are necessary in order for contributions, up to a certain amount (presently a maximum of $5,000 per beneficiary per year), to be treated present gifts for gift and estate tax purposes. Present gifts of up to $10,000 per beneficiary per year involve no gift tax consequences. Gifts of future interests in any amount, however, generally will create gift tax consequences. Crummey provisions, therefore, enable you to avoid any gift tax consequences. (3) Your spouse will have the power to appoint trust property (including a life insurance policy) to you or to your children. This creates some flexibility in this otherwise unchangeable and inflexible instrument. (4) At your death, the trustee will be able to use trust assets (such as cash from life insurance proceeds) either to purchase assets from your estate or to loan money to your estate. This enables the trust to provide liquidity to your estate for the payment of estate taxes and administrative expenses. (5) As with all trust documents, the trust should state what happens to the assets at your death, what the powers of the trustees are and under what circumstances, if any, the trustee can be replaced. The Super Trust can work wonders in keeping life insurance proceeds out of both your estate and your spouse's. This type of trust is an essential part of estate planning for most very large estates. It maximizes the benefits of life insurance and enables you to reduce your estate and still to control what happens to your property upon death.

In the case of an irrevocable trust, as with any life insurance purchase, it may be desirable that life insurance be purchased initially in a qualified plan to pay for front end costs with tax deductible plan contributions and then purchased from the qualified plan by the insured before the transfer to the irrevocable trust. This enables the owner to maximize the use of before-tax dollars and thereby to minimize his total acquisition costs of the insurance. In general, it does not make any sense for life insurance to continue to be owned in a qualified plan since the qualified plan proceeds are includable in the estate just as though they had been owned by the plan participant on a personal basis.

Occasionally, it may be desirable for life insurance to be owned by children where they are the ones who will be required to pay the death taxes. Also, where death taxes are concerned, sometimes a second to die life insurance policy is desirable since this is the time when life insurance proceeds are most needed to pay estate and other death taxes. Often, a second to die policy is acquired by a Super Trust.

Installment Payment of Taxes

If the decedent's interest in a closely held business meets or exceeds 20% of the adjusted gross estate (essentially the gross estate less deductions for estate expenses, indebtedness and taxes), the portion of the tax attributable to that interest may be paid in a maximum of 10 annual installments. In addition, the executor may elect to delay the beginning of the installment payments up to five years by making four annual payments of interest only. The interest will be 2% on the first $1,000,000 of closely held business interest for estates of decedents dying after January 1, 1998 (if the decedent dies before this date, the interest rate is 4%).

For purposes of determining whether an estate qualifies for this special installment payment treatment, the term "interest in a closely held business" means -

(A)an interest as a proprietor in a trade or business carried on as proprietorship;

(B)an interest as a partner in a partnership carrying on a trade or business, if -

(i) 20 percent or more of the total capital interest in such partnership is included in determining the gross estate of the decedent, or

(ii) such partnership had 15 or fewer partners; or

(C)stock in a corporation carrying on a trade or business if -

(i) 20 percent or more in value of the voting stock of such corporation is included in determining the gross estate of the decedent, or

(ii) such corporation had 15 or fewer shareholders.

The installment election terminates and the balance of the tax payable in installments has to be paid if (1) any portion of the business interest is distributed, sold, exchanged, or otherwise disposed of, or money and other property attributable to such an interest is withdrawn from the business, and (2) the aggregate of such distributions, sales, exchanges, or other dispositions and withdrawals equals or exceeds 50% of the value of such interest. Distribution to an heir is not counted as a distribution for this purpose.

Value Shifting Techniques

There are several techniques that large estates can use to save on federal estate taxes. Since these techniques involve the shifting of appreciation from one generation to the next they are referred to as value shifting techniques but can also be referred to as estate freezes.

While there are different opportunities available, we will discuss the three main concepts to create a flavor of what can be accomplished.

I. **Recapitalization.** If you own a closely held business interest, you might think of recapitalizing the company to create two classes of stock, a preferred class and a common class. The preferred class generally has a fixed value with a fixed dividend and should provide for a cumulative dividend meaning that if a dividend is skipped in one year it will be made up in a subsequent year. The preferred should be non-voting and carry an interest rate which is reflective of the risk involved as well as what the market place is currently paying. One approach would be to fix the interest at the current prime interest rate plus 2%, 3% or 4% or even higher depending on the risk of the investment.

In order for dividends from the preferred stock to qualify as qualified payments (you will want to check this with your counsel) it must be cumulative and determined (i) at a fixed rate or (ii) at a rate that bears a fixed relationship to a specified market interest rate. It is important for the preferred stock dividend to qualify as a qualified payment or else the preferred stock will be treated as having a zero value after the gift of the common is made. The importance of this cannot be overstated.

> **Example:** Jason recapitalizes his million dollar business and retains $500,000 of preferred with a 6% dividend, non-cumulative, and gives away the common stock to his son, Oscar. Because the preferred stock is determined to have a zero value, Jason's gift to Oscar is treated by the Internal Revenue Service as a gift of one million dollars.

The advantage, of course, of the recapitalization is the shifting of future appreciation from one generation to the next. Assuming that the preferred stock is properly set up, it causes a fixed value to remain with the older generation while transferring the opportunity for future appreciation to the younger generation.

> **Example:** David recapitalizes his $800,000 business by issuing $400,000 of preferred and then gives away the $400,000 of common to his son, Bradley. Under IRS regulations, the gift is determined by taking the total value of the company ($800,000) and subtracting from it the retained interest ($400,000) to result in the gift of $400,000. It is important in this case that the preferred stock bear an appropriate interest rate and that it be cumulative.

If the double taxation on the preferred stock dividends creates a problem for taxpayers they may want to consider a partnership setting for this type of estate freeze. The partnership will not cause the imposition of double taxation and is a valid technique with parents owning a fixed interest and children owning the interest that can appreciate.

II. **Qualified Personal Residence Trust.** A person can transfer a personal residence to a qualified personal residence trust (QPRT) for a term of years with the residence (at the end of the term) to then pass to the surviving spouse or to children. The advantage of this technique is that the ultimate gift to the children is discounted based on the term of the trust and the age of the grantor.

> **Example:** Thelma transferred her condominium with a value of $110,000 into a trust for 10 years with the beneficiary at the end of 10 years being her daughter. Based on the current interest rates in effect under published Internal Revenue Service Tables and based on Thelma's age of 71 at the time of setting up the qualified personal residence trust, she is deemed to make a gift to her daughter of only $27,723. The gift is reported on a current basis and consumes a portion of Thelma's $625,000 exemption equivalent. Even if the condominium has doubled in value in 10 years, the gift remains the same. Only if Thelma dies before the 10 years is up does the personal residence get added back to her estate.

Since many people would like to live in their personal residence for a long period of time before passing it on to children, the qualified personal residence trust is to some extent a win no lose situation. If the grantor survives for the term of the trust, then the property is transferred at a very favorable gift rate to the children. If the grantor dies before the term is up, then the residence is added back into the grantor's estate, very similar to the situation if nothing were done. Consequently, there is not much risk involved in setting up a qualified personal residence trust other than the attorney fees to do so.

Each person can do two qualified personal residence trusts during his or her lifetime. Generally, any property transferred to the trust can be sold and then the proceeds can be used to either purchase a new personal residence or it can be used to make payments to the grantor based on annuity trust rules.

The Taxpayer Relief Act of 1997 provides that certain individuals are able to exclude from taxable income up to $250,000 of gain ($500,000, in general, for married couples filing a joint return) realized on the sale of property that has been used as a principle residence. During the income term of the personal residence trust, the trust is taxed as a grantor trust. This means that the residence could be sold within the trust with the tax consequences of the sale passing through to you thereby enabling you to take advantage of the above described tax exclusion on the sale of the residence.

If you have a QPRT, you should at least consider the sale of the residence (even if it will be replaced with another residence) toward the end of the income term of the trust. This creates a greater basis in the property eventually passing to the trust beneficiaries. Please note that if the trust residence is sold, a portion of any cash held in the trust will be required to be distributed during the income term to the Grantor pursuant to IRS Regulations.

III. Grantor Retained Annuity Trusts. Under this type of trust, the grantor transfers property and retains an interest to a fixed percentage of the transferred property for a term of years. The amount of gift to the trust is based on the term of years as well as the retained interest. These are extremely popular trusts for high income producing situations.

> **Example:** Arnold, owner of A.J. Printing, Inc., transfers $450,000 cash to a 10 year GRAT paying 16% per year to Arnold. His children are beneficiaries. The $450,000 cash is used by Arnold's wife as trustee to purchase a building in an arms length transaction. The building is then leased to A.J. Printing for $72,000 per year pursuant to an appraisal which qualifies the $72,000 per year as fair rental for a 10 year period of time. Arnold retains the right of substitution of property in the trust so he gets all of the benefits of depreciation of the real estate. At the end of 10 years, the children receive the real estate and Arnold can continue to pay rent to them. In the alternative, Arnold can purchase the real estate himself from the trust and then the children can receive the cash or other property that is put into the trust by Arnold. In this example because of the high

interest payout for a 10 year period of time, Arnold is deemed to make a zero gift to his children. However, a gift tax return should be filed to report the transaction.

The Grantor retained annuity trust also works very well with closely held stock. A minority interest in stock can be discounted. Since S corporation stock can be put into a grantor retained annuity trust if certain conditions are met, including the possibility that the grantor can substitute property of equal value for the trust property, there are some excellent planning opportunities in family situations.

Example: Tom has a S corporation with a value of a million dollars that produces about $100,000 per year of income that passes through to him as taxable income. He has a son age 16 who he believes will be interested in the business and whom he wants to give significant stock ownership. He transfers 40% of his company to a grantor retained annuity trust for seven years paying back to him each year 20% of the value of the stock transferred. He has the stock appraised with a dis count applying of 50% for lack of marketability and minority interest and thereby is easily able to make the 20% payout based on current S corporation income. His gift is discounted to zero because of the very high payout and he is thereby able to trans fer a significant block of stock to his son without the imposition of any federal estate or gift taxes.

The grantor retained annuity trust is becoming increasing popular as attorneys and accountants become more familiar with its benefits and are more easily able to advise clients. It can be an important part of any type of value shifting planning.

Sales to a Grantor Trust

Under this planning, an individual establishes a special trust that is treated the same income tax-wise as the individual. This so-called "Grantor Trust" can then be used to purchase assets from the grantor in a way that is effective for estate taxes but neutral for income tax purposes.

Example: Albert owns 10 shares of voting common stock and 90 shares of non voting stock of B-Ball, Inc., an S-Corporation. While the entire corporation is worth $1 million, the 90 shares of non voting stock are appraised at only $500,000 based on dis counts for lack of marketability and lack of control.

Albert establishes a grantor trust that he funds with $60,000 cash. About two weeks later, the trustee of the trust purchases Albert's interest in the non voting shares for $600,000 using the $60,000 cash as a down payment and giving Albert a promissory note for $540,000. The note is paid to Albert by distribu tions received by the trust from the S-Corporation.

The trust can hold S-corporation stock because it is a grantor trust.

Family Business Relief Provisions

The 1997 Taxpayer Relief Act provides an important estate tax exemption for those of you in a family business. If you qualify, an exemption bonus for the value of your interest in your business is added to your unified credit exemption so that a maximum of $1.3 million may be excluded from estate tax.

The next question is, of course, what does it take to qualify? Some general requirements are the following. The value of your business must be more than half of your estate (as provided by the appropriate provisions of the Tax Code). During the eight years prior to your death, there must have been some material participation by either you or your family for at least five years. Additionally, your interest in the business must pass to close members of your family (as provided by the Tax Code and held by them for 10 years). Finally, if you own the business with other families, you must own a larger portion of the business to qualify as provided by the Tax Code.

Avoiding Probate

A number of books have been written about how to avoid probate. They suggest there can be tremendous savings by maneuvering attorneys and our court system out of probate matters. There is some truth to this but you need to hear the rest of the story.

Probate is simply the process of settling an individual's estate. The mechanism of estate settlement involves ascertaining the net assets of the estate and distributing the assets to the heirs. More specifically, probate consists of (1) identifying, appraising and reporting all assets of the deceased; (2) identifying and paying all estate debts; (3) filing tax returns; (4) paying attorney's fees, probate court fees, and executor's fees; and (5) distributing property according to the terms of the deceased's will, and if there is no will, according to state statute. Assets that (a) are given away in one's lifetime; (b) pass according to contract (such as through joint ownership or as life insurance proceeds); or (c) are placed in a lifetime trust are not subject to probate.

In order to avoid probate, you only need to do one of the three things mentioned above. The transfer of assets to trusts is one of the most common approaches taken to avoid probate, but it has certain drawbacks. Tax returns must be filed for the trust and property must be held and transferred in the trust's name. It often is more time consuming and vexatious to work with trust ownership and trust returns than is worth the effort.

Another very common technique is to have all assets owned by husband and wife jointly with a right of survivorship. On the first death, the surviving spouse takes over all ownership of assets without having to go through the probate process. This technique never should be used if federal estate tax is a concern, because the full value of all jointly held assets will be included in both estates for federal estate tax purposes.

The avoidance of probate can be over-emphasized. People who have large estates need to be first and foremost concerned about federal estate taxes. If they make avoidance of probate a primary concern, it can cause them to lose sight of a much more important issue and that is their federal estate tax liability. For people who do not have a federal estate tax problem, the avoidance of probate can be a desirable and worthwhile pursuit. It makes especially good sense for someone who has a terminal illness to take steps to avoid probate since probate can be costly and time consuming.

Gift Giving

Gift giving can be an important part of estate planning. An individual can give up to $10,000 (indexed for inflation beginning in 1999) per person per year without incurring any gift or estate tax consequences. Husband and wife together can combine to give $20,000 in gifts in one year to an individual. Starting in 1999, this per person amount will be increased by an inflation adjustment that tracks the consumer price index. Also, if the statute of limitations period (usually three years) has passed on the gift, the gift can not be revalued by the IRS for the purpose of determining the available unified credit and the applicable estate tax bracket.

If a person wants to give away a large sum of money and yet earmark who that money will eventually go to, the use of the Crummey trust which has been discussed above for life insurance can be very advantageous. The Crummey trust permits gifts per beneficiary per year of up to $5,000. If an individual, age 85, for example, has four children, 12 grandchildren, and 20 great grandchildren, the 85 year old individual may make gift and estate tax free gifts to a Crummey trust of $5,000 times 36 or $180,000 per year. All of the named designated beneficiaries have to have the right of withdrawal of a pro-rata portion of the gift, but for purposes of planning, it is important that they not exercise their withdrawal right. The trust can be set up so that even though all the beneficiaries have the right of withdrawal, upon the death of the grantor the assets of the trust will pass to the grantor's children, if they in fact are who he wants to have all of the assets. This can be a very effective technique of gift giving and is one that is often overlooked for elderly people who need to be concerned about federal estate taxes.

In large estate situations, it can be desirable for taxable gifts to be made in order to pass future appreciation of property to other family members without the appreciation being subject to estate taxes.

Charitable Giving

We've discussed some charitable giving ideas in the chapter on income tax planning. In addition to reviewing in regard to gift and estate taxation the charitable remainder annuity trust and charitable lead trust that we discussed before, we will present here two other ideas involving trusts, the charitable remainder unitrust and the pooled income fund.

The charitable remainder unitrust is essentially the same as the charitable remainder annuity trust except the sum that is paid each year to the donor or the designated beneficiary is a stated percentage of the assets (not less than 5 percent of the annual value). The payments, like the annuity trust, can be limited to the actual income earned. Because payments from the trust increase as the value of the trust assets increase, the charitable remainder unitrust will generate higher payments than would an annuity trust, provided the trust assets are invested properly. Also, unlike the annuity trust, the unitrust does permit additional contributions in future years.

Example: In 1998 Donna, age 54, transferred a block of Procter and Gamble stock worth $100,000 to a charitable remainder unitrust for the benefit of her and her husband (age 55). They had a low cost basis in the stock and were uncomfortable selling it and reinvesting the proceeds. They set up the trust to pay out 8% of the trust corpus determined as of the beginning of each year to them for the rest of their lives. The stock could then be sold within the unitrust without Donna paying any capital gains taxes and the proceeds of the stock reinvested in a more diverse portfolio. Donna and her husband, in addition to avoiding the tax on the sale of the stock, also were entitled to an income tax deduction in excess of $10,000. **NOTE:** In this case Donna and her husband could name a private foundation as an alternate beneficiary of the charitable remainder unitrust. However, the opportunity to do this with publicly traded stock in a charitable remainder unitrust expires after June 1998 unless extended by Congress.

Note: Gifts to charities must be at least 10% of assets transferred.

A pooled income fund is a fund maintained by a public charity, which pays out to the donors each year a prorated portion of the income earned by the fund. The pooled income fund can not invest in tax exempt securities. Upon the death of the donor, the assets inure to the benefit of charity.

With any of the trust ideas, a contribution to the trust not only gives rise to a current charitable income tax deduction, but also keeps the assets that have been contributed out of the individual's estate.

The charitable lead trust, which provides income to the charity with a reversion to the donor or other designated beneficiary, can be used in estate planning in a very effective way. If an individual who sets up the charitable lead trust names a son or daughter as the ultimate beneficiary, the assets contributed to the charitable lead trust give rise not only to a current income tax deduction, but also can result in a substantial transfer that will be gift and estate tax free to the designated heir.

The charitable lead trust is a popular device for the taxpayer who has an unusually high income year and is willing to accept some income loss in future years to gain the benefit of a large income tax deduction in the current year. Assuming a five year trust that distributes nine percent each year of the contribution, the donor is entitled to an income tax deduction of about 46 percent of the contribution.

The charitable lead trust can also be set up as part of an individual's will since an estate tax deduction is allowed for the actuarial value of the income interest provided by the trust. For example, suppose an individual leaves $500,000 in trust to pay $30,000 to his favorite charity for 24 years (remainder to his children). This person's estate would be entitled to an estate tax deduction of over

$375,000. By setting annuity payments at a high enough level or making the payments for a sufficient duration, the individual could completely eliminate the tax on his bequest to the charitable lead trust. This again, is a very important estate planning technique for the very wealthy.

Generation Skipping

Gifts or bequests that skip a generation (such as a gift to a grandchild) are subject to a generation skipping tax. Each transferor is permitted a total of $1,000,000 for these types of transfers. The total amount for husband and wife is $2,000,000. Starting in 1999, this per person exemption amount will be increased by an inflation adjustment, in multiples of $10,000, based on the consumer price index. Any transfer in excess of this exemption is subject to any regular gift or estate tax plus an added tax at the highest gift and estate tax rate.

Exception: Under the "predeceased parent exception," an amount can be transferred directly to a grandchild without triggering the generation skipping tax if the if the child of the transferor who was the grandchild's parent is diseased at the time of the transfer. The 1997 Taxpayer Relief Act extends this exception to collateral heirs if the decedent has no living lineal decendents at the time of transfer. It is also extended to taxable terminations and distributions if the parent of the relevant beneficiary was dead at the earliest time that the transfer was subject to estate or gift tax. This special exemption, plus the $1,000,000 per transferor exemption described above enables significant gifts to be made to grandchildren. However, planning must be done to take advantage of the exemption.

Medicaid Planning

One of the big concerns individuals have is preserving assets for the next generation. With nursing home expenses on the horizon for so many of the elderly, there is a whole branch of law that has developed that has to do with planning to be eligible to receive medicaid payments.

There is a thirty-six (36) month period prior to being eligible for medicaid when all gifts that have been made during that period of time are added back into the applicant's net worth. Generally, in order to qualify for medicaid, the net worth of an individual must be below a threshold amount. Consequently, it is very common for parents to make gifts to children or enter into other types of planning mechanisms to avoid holding large assets in the event of nursing home needs. But these gifts need to be made thirty-six (36) months or more before medicaid eligibility for nursing home expenses is requested

In addition to making gifts to children, parents may establish an irrevocable trust that pays out income only to the parents with principal distributed to the children. In the worst possible case situation, the children could then receive principal and make gifts back to the parents as needed. However, in order to establish this kind of irrevocable trust, it should be established at least sixty (60) months prior to a possible nursing home need.

Estate Planning in Community Property States

There are nine states which are community property states: Arizona, California, Idaho, Louisiana, Nevada, New Mexico, Texas, Washington and Wisconsin. These states base ownership of property on the general theory that husband and wife form a partnership and own equally the property acquired during their marriage, unless there is some specific agreement to the contrary. Some special estate tax planning steps have to be taken in community property states, which include having one spouse acquiesce in the transfer of property, including life insurance policies, in which separate ownership interests have been established.

ESTATE PLANNING CHECKLIST

EVERYONE NEEDS:

Current Will - containing appointment of executor (and one or more back-ups), specific bequests, dispositive provisions and broad powers for executor.

FOR PEOPLE WITH MINOR CHILDREN OR OTHER DEPENDENTS

Review life insurance coverage; need revocable inter-vivos trust to hold assets in event of death of one or both parents.

Trust provides basis on which assets will be held, invested and distributed. Trust should be document separate from Will with nominal funding ($10) during lifetime.

FOR MARRIED COUPLES WITH MORE THAN $625,000 IN TOTAL ASSETS AT DEATH INCLUDING INSURANCE PROCEEDS

Should have a marital deduction trust which provides for the creation of a family and marital trust so that no estate taxes will be paid at the first death and minimal estate taxes will be paid at the second death.

Family trust should provide for possible distributions of income to other family members and ability to accumulate income within the trust to take advantage of possible lower trust tax bracket.

FOR SINGLE INDIVIDUALS WITH MORE THAN $625,000 IN TOTAL ASSETS (INCLUDING INSURANCE) AND MARRIED COUPLES WITH MORE THAN $1.250 MILLION IN ASSETS (INCLUDING INSURANCE)

Should have an irrevocable trust to provide for life insurance proceeds to pass in a way that will not be subject to estate taxation at death. Trust should include certain withdrawal rights for beneficiaries ("Crummey powers") and provide, in most cases, for distribution of assets in same way as family trust.

FOR ANYONE STILL IN ABOVE CATEGORY AFTER EXCLUDING INSURANCE PROCEEDS, CONSIDER

Gift program through trust ($5000 limit per year for each beneficiary who has withdrawal rights) or direct to individuals ($10,000 gift limit for each donee per year - husband and wife can combine for $20,000 gift per donee per year).

Installment sale to transfer appreciating property to next generation at fixed price.

Private annuity to shift tax from federal estate tax rate of up to 55% to long term capital gains rate of maximum of 28% (1987) or 33% thereafter.

Sale of a private annuity so that property will pass at death free of estate taxes.

Creation of family partnership (used primarily for real estate) to transfer appreciation to next generation.

Establishing a qualified personal residence trust and a grantor trust

CHAPTER 12
THE ELEMENTS OF FINANCIAL PLANNING

Everyone does some financial planning. If you keep track of income and expenses, save money and make investments, you are doing the basics of financial planning. Yet, a common problem with financial planning is that it is done on a piecemeal basis.

One of the most important parts of financial planning is identifying your financial goals and how to achieve them. Recently, a client came to us with a movie tax shelter that he had purchased without the advice of either an accountant or an attorney. He was concerned because he had a very large note that had to be paid after nine years and because the film had not been delivered to his distributor for marketing. Furthermore, he entered into the movie partnership in a year when the tax benefits were too large to be used fully at his level of income. As you can imagine, it was expensive and time consuming for him to work his way out of a program that might have been a justifiable risk for someone else, but was not beneficial for him.

If this were a one-time occurrence, it would be easy to discount. However, I have seen other programs that individuals have entered into without the proper planning or professional review on the very general theory that the program sounded advantageous. Any tax oriented investment should generally be reviewed by the investment adviser, accountant and attorney. Furthermore, financial planning is much more than simply having the proper advice for entering into investments. It is a process of living in a financially responsible manner and accumulating wealth through the different passages of life.

The Basic Steps of Financial Planning

On Monday, December 2, 1985 the Wall Street Journal published a special report on financial planning. On page 16D of that report appeared an advertisement by the International Association for Financial Planners that presented the fundamentals of financial planning in such a clear way that we have taken the liberty of quoting most of it:

Six Steps

There are six specific steps in the financial planning process. This process ensures that your financial plan covers all the bases.

1. *Collect and Assess all Relevant Data.* Starting with your first visit, a financial planner helps you gather documents, asks questions, and gets to know you. You work with a planner to gather the facts and figures to pin down your financial position now.
2. *Identify Personal Financial Goals.* You know the things you want. A financial planner can help you translate them into specific objectives that are measurable in dollars and cents.
3. *Identify Financial Problems.* Your planner focuses on specific problems that stand in the way of your goals, such as inadequate cash flow, for example, or excessive tax payments. Or the wrong kinds of insurance and investments.
4. *Provide Written Recommendations and Alternative Solutions.* A good financial plan shows you, step by step, specific actions to take and offers a variety of alternatives.
5. *Implement or Coordinate Implementation.* Your financial planner can help you put your plan into action. He or she can assist you in implementing the plan or, if you prefer, work with other specialists.
6. *Review and Revise Your Plan Periodically.* Your planner should periodically review your plan and make necessary revisions where needed. He or she should update your plan to account for changes in your life, in current economic conditions or in tax laws.

This six step process is fundamental to planning for and achieving financial success. Let's now take a look at some of the things people want to achieve financially.

Typical Goals

Typical goals for an individual may include any or all of the following:

1. Financial independence by attainment of age 60.
2. Accumulation of sufficient funds to help children pay for a college education.
3. Investment of assets in a manner that will provide for protection against a return of high inflation and high interest rates.
4. An overall strategy to minimize tax liability and to accumulate wealth.
5. Minimization of federal estate taxes.
6. Financial protection for the family in the event of a premature death or a serious illness.

It is only through establishing goals that it becomes possible to achieve financial success. Goal setting and goal monitoring enable us to maintain positive movement in a financial plan and to make the most of the effort and expense that will go into consulting with the professionals we need.

Monitoring Your Net Worth

The driving component behind wealth accumulation is cash flow management. With proper cash flow management we can add significantly to our accumulation of wealth each year. But the real measure of where we are financially right now is our net worth statement. As such, calculating net worth is an integral part of the financial planning process. Net worth is essentially the difference between total assets and total liabilities. The calculation of net worth gives us valuable information about the investment assets we have to work with in the future.

A form of calculating net worth is included at the end of this chapter. With this form you can determine the following:

- the investment assets available to your family in the event of your death (exclusive of insurance proceeds);
- the relationship between your liquid and non-liquid investments;
- the relative percentage of your assets in each of the three major investment categories;
- the degree of leverage in your investment portfolio, i.e. the relationship between your investments and your liabilities;
- the net investments available for current expenditures (such as education) or the creation of cash flow at retirement. (To project the value at retirement, multiply current net investments by the appropriate compound interest factor set forth in Chapter 10, Pathway Number Seven); and
- the size of your estate for estate planning purposes (add to net worth the face amount of life insurance in excess of cash value for any policies on your life in which you have any ownership rights)

These determinations are essential for monitoring where you stand with each of the Eight Pathways. Because of the importance of having access to the above information, you should calculate your net worth at least once each year. This will enable you to measure your financial progress against the goals you have set for yourself in each of the Eight Pathways.

Importance of Implementation

One area of the financial planning process that is deserving of special attention is the area of implementation. After the analysis and goal setting comes the implementation. Without implementing the plans that have been made, the whole process will be for naught.

A large bank in the southwestern United States recently did financial planning for top executives in a local company. The process seemed to be going along fine until the bank planners went back for an annual review; they found the people were less than enthusiastic in talking with them. Only twenty percent of the planners' recommendations had been executed and as a result, the executives had not made much progress. Consequently, financial planning for these executives had not been worthwhile. Why? Because no one had been charged with the responsibility of seeing that the recommendations were executed.

Simply going through the planning steps does not guarantee you will achieve or even begin to achieve your financial goals. Whether or not you hire a financial planner to assist you, you will need to assign to one person the responsibility to follow through with you on the implementation of the plans you have made for each of the eight pathways. This then brings us to the role of professionals in helping you achieve your desired financial success.

Calculation of Net Worth

Assets:	**Value**	**%**
Liquid Assets		
Cash (checking, savings accounts)	____________	_______
Money Market Funds	____________	_______
Cash Value of Life Insurance	____________	_______
Other	____________	_______
OTHER Low Risk, Low Return Assets		
Personal Residence	____________	_______
High Grade Corporate Bonds	____________	_______
Municipal Bonds	____________	_______
Government Securities	____________	_______
Other	____________	_______
TOTAL L.R., L.R.	____________	_______

Moderate Risk, Moderate Return Assets		
Real Estate	________	______
Managed Portfolio	________	______
Mutual Funds	________	______
"Junk" Corporate Bonds	________	______
Convertible Bonds	________	______
Other	________	______
TOTAL M.R., M.R.	________	______
High Risk, High Return Assets		
Individual Stocks	________	______
Venture Capital Funds	________	______
Oil and Gas Ventures	________	______
Equipment Leases	________	______
Gold and other Precious Metals	________	______
Other	________	______
TOTAL H.R., H.R.	________	______

Liabilities:

Short Term		
Borrowings on Life Insurance	________	______
Installment Loans	________	______
Personal Loans	________	______
Accrued Taxes	________	______
Other	________	______
TOTAL Short Term Liabilities	________	______
Long Term		
Home Mortgage	________	______
First	________	______
Second	________	______
Other Real Estate Mortgages	________	______
Loans to Purchase Investment Assets	________	______
TOTAL Long Term Liabilities	________	______

TOTAL LIABILITIES	________	______
NET INVESTMENT ASSETS (ASSETS - LIABILITIES)	________	______

Personal Assets:

Home Furnishings	________	______
Automobiles	________	______
Art, Antiques	________	______
Boat	________	______
Other	________	______
TOTAL Personal Assets	________	______
NET WORTH (Net Investment Assets + Personal Assets)	________	______

CHAPTER 13
THE ROLE OF PROFESSIONALS IN FINANCIAL PLANNING

Planning for financial success requires assistance from the following professionals: tax accountant, tax attorney, life underwriter, investment advisor (or stockbroker) for stocks, bonds, equities, limited partnerships and other investments, and someone (who may be one of the above) who functions as the financial planner (i.e., the person who pulls everything together and helps give the program a sense of direction). In general, the more the professionals complement one another in the financial planning process, the more effective the financial plan will be for the recipient.

Commonly, life insurance agents or stockbrokers call themselves financial planners. These professionals often perform financial planning services in a very productive fashion. But be aware that occasionally financial planning can be used as an inducement to the purchase of a product by the client. As you can imagine, in such a situation, the financial planning process can be deprived of needed objectivity.

The ideal would seem to be to work with a financial planner who has only his time to sell. Financial planning, however, is a new concept and most of the people who are involved in financial planning do sell product. If the best person available to you does so, you should establish early in the relationship at what point he may recommend that you purchase his product. This will give you a position from which to monitor his performance in setting a well balanced plan with goals in many different areas and not just in the area in which he has product to sell.

The roles of the different professionals identified above requires some definition. The importance of the definition should be apparent. You do not want professionals to give you advice in areas in which they do not have proper training. For example, you do not want your attorney to give you investment advice. Similarly, you should not look to your life underwriter for legal advice, nor would you want your investment advisor to have the final say on your tax planning.

Proper Professional Roles

1. **FINANCIAL PLANNER**

The financial planner is the quarterback of the team that helps the client plan for financial success. He follows each of the six steps set forth in the previous chapter. He collects the data, helps set goals, assists in developing plans to achieve the goals, brings in other professionals or sees that the client works with his own professionals, makes sure each plan is implemented, and monitors the plans to determine if the goals are being achieved. Any of the professionals discussed below could function as the financial planner. You may be able to function as your own financial planner if you pursue the direction given by this book and employ the professionals necessary to help you achieve your goals.

2. **TAX ACCOUNTANT**

The tax accountant determines if the data collected by the planner are accurate, makes whatever complex tax projections are needed, such as whether the alternative minimum tax may come into effect; helps evaluate the appropriateness of certain proposed investments, especially those investments such as limited partnership investments, which carry with them substantial tax characteristics; and, very importantly, monitors the investments that have been made to see that they are performing on schedule. The tax accountant must consider the tax oriented investments in light of the client's tax situation for this kind of investment to gain its full value.

Recently, many accountants have begun to call themselves financial planners. In many respects, this is a reasonable role for the accountant to play and more and more accountants will hold themselves out as financial planners in the future. Accountants who become financial planners must become accustomed to working with other professionals to implement the financial plan.

3. **TAX ATTORNEY**

The tax attorney is the final authority for the review, interpretation and preparation of all legal documents including wills and trusts. Also, he should be involved in the implementation of various tax planning techniques, such as preparing trusts to help build up funds for college education, determining the value of certain partnership investments, and finding tax efficient ways to purchase life insurance. The tax attorney should advise the client on legal matters pertaining to financial planning and should be used as a source of advice on various investment programs.

4. **LIFE UNDERWRITER**

The life underwriter reviews, evaluates and makes recommendations concerning the areas of life insurance, disability insurance, and health insurance. The life underwriter should frequently review the client's insurance needs to determine if the types and amounts of insurance owned by the client are appropriate. To the extent necessary, the life underwriter may also need to bring in a casualty and property insurance agent to help review the client's casualty and property insurance. Casualty insurance coverage is extremely important in this day and age of very high jury awards in personal injury cases.

5. **INVESTMENT ADVISOR**

The investment advisor may actually consist of three different people — and perhaps more. The client needs an investment advisor for his conservative investments, for his moderate risk investments with a little higher rate of return, and for his high risk, high return investments. In this era of specialization, it is unusual for one person adequately to meet the diverse investment needs that are represented by the three different investment areas.

The fact that someone holds himself out as a registered advisor means very little. The display of Securities and Exchange Commission ("SEC") registration only proves that the advisor has completed a short form and paid the SEC a modest fee. As is true with hiring any professional, seek the advice of other professionals or satisfied clients before selecting an investment advisor.

A registered investment advisor may be very reluctant to offer advice on anything other than the specific program in which the client is enrolled. A client who has additional money to invest may choose to employ more than one registered investment advisor or to work with a stockbroker for some of his investments and a registered investment advisor for others.

Many investment advisors require a minimum investment of $100,000 in order to offer investment advice and charge between .5% and 2% of the principal on a yearly basis for their advice. In addition, a brokerage fee will have to be paid for the execution of the recommendations that are made.

6. STOCKBROKERS

Stockbrokers aka account executives and financial consultants have access to many tremendous investment opportunities some of which work better than others. Because the broker primarily makes his living out of the commissions he receives from buying and selling securities, some brokers can become over zealous in recommending how frequently trades occur in an account.

A good broker can be extremely useful as a sounding board, as a provider of information, and, because of his knowledge, with the mechanics of buying and selling. Also, unquestionably some brokers give good advice, often by steering clients away from obvious bad ideas. But there are substantial differences in the quality of brokers. By way of examples, some are always there and some are not, some make very sound recommendations while others push whatever their firm desires, some can take orders and get quotes rapidly and others take several minutes, and some have competent assistants who can handle most matters when the broker isn't available. Also, if an investor deals in some special area, such as options, it pays to have a broker who is experienced in that area.

Most individuals begin their investment life with a retail stockbroker. Consider working with a stockbroker who comes highly recommended by a friend or a professional advisor. Also, it may be advisable to interview more than one stockbroker to determine investment philosophy. Go to the interview with a rough financial statement to make the meeting as productive as possible. Finally, do not be reluctant to talk with the manager of the local office to get his recommendations of who in his office would be best for you and your situation.

If you like to be your own investment advisor and have final say over where your money is invested, you probably should work with a stockbroker rather than a registered investment advisor. When you employ an investment advisor, you relinquish control over how your money is invested.

Evalution of Team Professionals

The financial planner (or you if you are your own financial planner) should review with the client the different professionals that need to be involved. To the extent possible, the client should be very clear on who is doing what for him. Furthermore, either the financial planner or the client should maintain contact with the various professionals to prevent overlap by one professional into areas outside of his area of expertise. This is the best way to insure that the client gets the best advice from the available resources and does not rely on any one person for advice in all areas.

Once the financial planning team is assembled in full, each member should know what each members' responsibilities are and be prepared to call on these professionals for their advice.

Personal Financial Planning Team

1. Financial Planner ____________________
2. Tax Accountant ____________________
3. Tax Attorney ____________________
4. Life Underwriter ____________________
5. Investment Adviser ____________________
6. Stockbroker ____________________

This list should be given to each team member.

CHAPTER 14
FINANCIAL PLANNING IN BALANCE

Things which matter most must be at the mercy of things which matter least.

Goethe

We have presented the eight fundamental areas of planning for financial success along with some information on the elements of financial planning, selecting advisors, and the psychology of success. Now we are ready to develop a process for monitoring our goals and objectives.

Why Balance in Financial Planning is Important

Joe (not his true name) is a high powered, dynamic guy whom everyone loves. He is a very successful professional who until recently has had trouble accumulating significant wealth. Joe has been a big consumer who has traveled in the fast lane, owning a very expensive home and several foreign cars. Joe has had an aggressive retirement plan to shelter big income dollars but has had very little cash to invest on a personal basis.

Recently, Joe has had such extreme success in his business that even he has been unable to consume all the income. In addition, he has broken the habit of buying new cars regularly. He seems to have become interested in wealth accumulation. The only thing that has happened to make this difficult is that Joe now is talking about slowing down and even retiring. This doesn't make a whole lot of sense because Joe is in his early 40s and is right at the top of his profession.

Most people find it easier to develop discipline with regard to savings than to work harder and more productively to increase income dramatically. If financial planning is done in balance, no time need come when an individual burns out vocationally. An individual's vocation should become more exciting and more interesting as he grows and develops as a professional and business person. Yet some people race so hard for so long that they experience burn out and lose interest in what they are doing at the first sign of having a bit of money set aside.

Planning for financial success is more durable if it consists of a disciplined approach to the achievement of long term goals and objectives. It doesn't make sense for a person to run so hard in one direction that he gets tired and chooses to slow down. It is not quite the same as the story of the tortoise and the hare but that story sticks with us because it is so true - that a slow plodder often does better in the long run than the person who is out to become an overnight success.

The key aspect to planning for success is balance. Without balance in an individual's financial life, serious problems can develop. If you exercise balance across the pathways of financial success, you can take pleasure in measuring the returns on your efforts on a regular basis.

Prioritizing Financial Goals

Establishing financial goals is a process that is similar to any goal setting. As an example, we will start with the typical financial goals set forth in chapter 11 and prioritize those goals by asking some basic questions about what is most important to us and what we intend to do about it. This process automatically results in financial planning. Because your answers to the basic questions may differ from those given in the example, your plans may differ also. A framework is presented at the end of this chapter for your to use for your own prioritization.

WHAT IS MOST IMPORTANT?

Financial protection for family in the event of death or serious illness.

WHY?

Because we do not want our dreams to die with us in the event of a premature death, or to become impossible in the event of a long illness or disability.

WHAT DO WE NEED TO DO?

Determine how much health, disability and life insurance is enough. Budget for the expense and pay in the most tax efficient way possible. Work with a quality agent to help assess needs and the best manner of payment. If in doubt, obtain competitive bids.

WHAT IS SECOND MOST IMPORTANT?

Accumulation of funds to help children pay for college.

WHY?

A college education can help our children grow and become financially independent. Making the commitment to do our share sets a good example and should help motivate our children to do their share.

WHAT DO WE NEED TO DO?

Calculate how much will be needed for college and what share we desire to provide. Establish a yearly objective to meet this long term goal. If possible, employ children in our business. Consider gift and leaseback, but only for children 14 and over. For children under 14, make sufficient gifts either to a custodial account or to a minor's trust to generate the $1,000 of income subject to favorable tax treatment.

WHAT IS THE THIRD MOST IMPORTANT?

Financial independence by age 60.

WHY?

Part of our life plan might be to allow for travel, hobbies, and spending time with our family. Age 60 is young enough for most people to be able fully to enjoy leisure time. Yet it is old enough to have provided the opportunity for sufficient wealth accumulation to have the choice of whether to work and if so, how hard.

WHAT DO WE NEED TO DO?

Calculate, based on today's standard of living, how much annual income would be required at age 60 to maintain an equivalent lifestyle. Determine what total amount will be needed to provide that income and how much must be set aside monthly to provide this amount. Budget for these monthly savings and develop a balanced portfolio of investments.

WHAT IS THE FOURTH MOST IMPORTANT?

Invest in a manner that provides protection against a return to high interest rates and high inflation.

WHY?

We do not want our investment portfolio to be too vulnerable to the whims of the financial indexes. We have learned that high inflation and high interest rates can be devastating - but we have also learned high inflation and high interest can be parlayed into some substantial gains.

WHAT DO WE NEED TO DO?

Assess our tolerance to risk as discussed in chapter 7 and analyze the balance in our portfolio. If we believe high inflation may return soon we need to consider increasing our investment in real estate. If we believe high interest rates will also return, we should consider (1) refinancing our home with a fixed rate mortgage, (2) staying liquid to take advantage of high interest rates, and (3) delaying any investment in long term fixed return investments such as municipal bonds, certificates of deposit and annuities.

The Wheel of Progress

The concept of a wheel of progress or balance wheel was initially presented in the author's book *Living Gangbusters* and is used

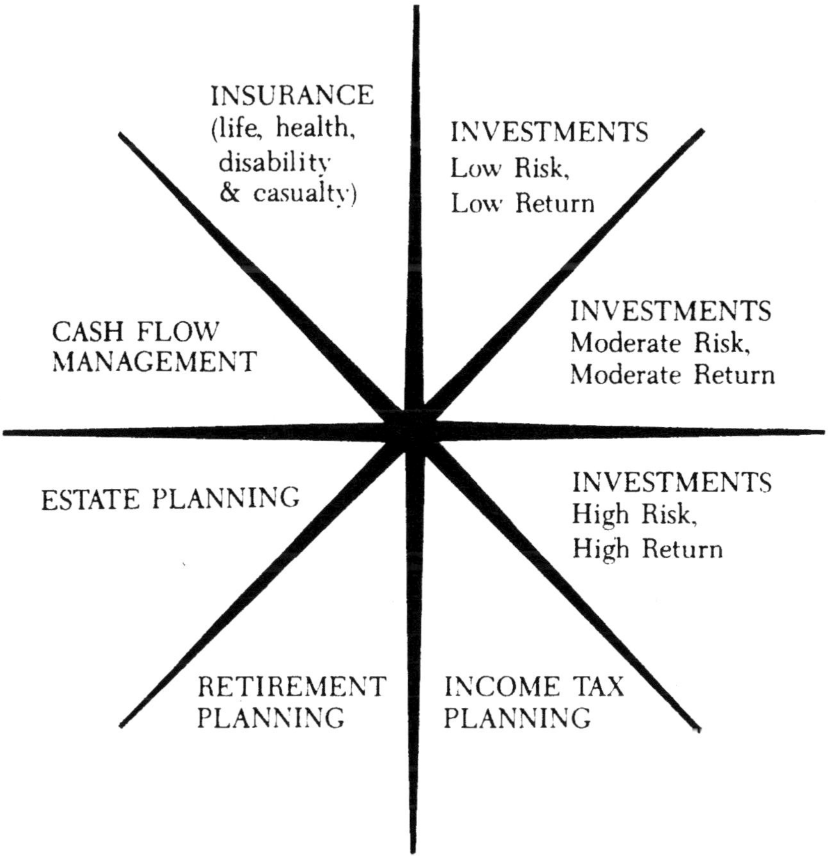
INSURANCE
(life, health,
disability
& casualty)
INVESTMENTS
Low Risk,
Low Return
CASH FLOW
MANAGEMENT
INVESTMENTS
Moderate Risk,
Moderate Return
ESTATE PLANNING
INVESTMENTS
High Risk,
High Return
RETIREMENT
PLANNING
INCOME TAX
PLANNING

Figure 14.1

with regard to becoming a life master in the last chapter of the book. The wheel of progress can be applied to the area of financial planning. The wheel of progress is shown in Figure 14.1 and should be reproduced so that it can be used frequently.

One suggestion is that the wheel of progress be used each month so that you can monitor how closely you are following your plans. The wheel of progress is used in the following manner:

1. In each area grade yourself on a scale of 1 to 10 for how successful you have been in following your plans to achieve your goals. Imagine 10 concentric circles and draw a partial circle corresponding to your score for each of the eight pathways. If you haven't even set goals in that area, t hen you should grade yourself four or less. If you have set goals that you have already met, give yourself a high score and then set new goals.
2. When you are done grading yourself, it will probably be apparent there are some areas in which you simply are not doing as well as in other areas.
3. Then make plans for how you will improve the area or areas in which you gave yourself a low grade and bring them up to the same high level as your other areas.

The concept here is an important one. Without balance in financial planning, we can become so committed to one area that we forget about the totality of what it is we are trying to achieve. For example, you do not want to overcommit funds to insurance products when you should be warehousing funds for retirement on a diversified basis. You want to have a balanced approach to both insurance and retirement. This is the concept that will get you the furthest in the long run.

Once you have begun the financial wheel of progress, be sure to keep records of where you have been and what progress you have made. This will enable you to develop confidence in the process you are using to achieve financial success.

Framework for Identifying Values and Action Plans to Achieve Them

1) What is most important to you in your financial life? _______

____

2) Why? ______________________________________

____

____

3) What do you need to do to improve what is most important to you? ___________________________________

____

____

____

4) What is next most important to you? ________________

5) Why? ______________________________________

____

6) What do you need to do to improve what is the second most important thing to you? __________________________

____

____

____

AND SO ON

CHAPTER 15
BECOMING A LIFE MASTER OF THE FINANCIAL GAME

Confucius say: Man who count happiness in dollars and cents must read financial sheet to see how happy he feel.

The previous chapters have introduced you to the tools you need to become a financial success. With these tools you can develop clear goals based on your own financial value system, establish plans to achieve those goals, hire competent professionals where needed, and use the balance wheel to monitor your progress.

But there is more to becoming a life master of the financial game than simply becoming a financial success. The financial game is just part of the life process. To become a life master we need to keep financial matters in balance with the other main areas of our lives. What good is it for you to be working your way to financial riches if the rest of your life is coming apart at the seams?

If You Had One Wish ...

Let's pretend for a moment that a genie has jumped out of a bottle and has offered to grant you one thing for the rest of your life. The options he gives you are the following:wealth, peace of mind, fame, or power. Which do you select?

People who have lived a long time generally select peace of mind. The reason for this is that with peace of mind, we can have a happy and satisfying life whether or not we have any or all of the other characteristics. How we think and feel about ourselves is much more important than how much wealth we amass during our lifetimes. In fact, the real riches in life have much more to do with our friendships, family, and virtues then they have to do with wealth, fame, or power.

Planning for financial success must be kept in perspective among the other aspects of an individual's life and should not have an overwhelming significance. If financial planning does not fit in a balanced way with an individual's other activities, it can become a negative rather than a positive factor. Once it becomes a negative, it becomes a burden rather than a joy and follow through can become very difficult.

Living in Balance

Focal Points for Our Life

Henry Van Dyke said, "Be glad of life because it gives you the chance to love and to work and to play and to look at the stars." To expand on his thinking, we can actually identify eight areas of our nature as human beings deserving individual attention at least some of the time. These areas are physical, emotional, social, educational, vocational, spiritual, financial, and recreational. Identification of these areas can help us achieve balance in our lives.

Physical

What are we doing to maintain our bodies? This isn't simply an issue of living as long as possible-who knows, a commercial flight, such as the one on which this chapter was first drafted, may not land-but it's an issue of living as well as we can for as long as we live. The better we feel, the better we live. The physical side of our life requires exercise, a balanced diet, and enjoying our sexual nature.

Ronald Reagan ran for reelection at age 73, an age at which most people are retired and savoring their golden years. In the last year of his first term, he looked in better health than when he took office. People who face challenges and who consistently look forward and attempt to improve generally stay in better health than those who do not. Lyndon Johnson suffered a serious heart attach in 1955, yet he served five years of the Presidency without serious additional complications. When he retired, he seemed to lose interest in life, reverted to harmful eating and smoking habits, and died four years later. Our bodies are only in as good a shape as our mental outlook.

Emotional

Are we excited about being alive? Do we feel we are living an ideal kind of life or just kind of roughing it until the big break comes along? The emotional component of our life is extremely important. In some ways it's our life report card. People who live successfully receive high marks and feel good about themselves. We add to our emotional growth by doing fun things, like going to movies, baseball games, or making love. Our emotional side also requires exercising control over potentially destructive feelings like anger and hate. We feel better about ourselves when we're constantly loving and giving people. Acting out of anger or hate does not help us or anyone else feel better. Also, our emotional well-being is increased by regular relaxation.

Social

How often do we do things with our friends and how freely do we give them love? Do we frequently make new friends so we have a wide variety of people with whom to share our experiences? It may be easier to put our immediate family first to the exclusion of other loved ones. But by feeding the loving and growing process with our friends, our lives are enriched. By giving unconditional love to others, we develop more tolerance for our own shortcomings and are better able to love ourselves unconditionally. The social component requires a natural addition of new friends. Giving unconditional love to others can be expressed through our commitment to charitable giving. Social activity and charitable dedication go hand in hand.

Educational

Is your knowledge of yourself and of the world around you growing? Education is a never-ending process. There are always valuable things to learn. Only the inexperienced foresake the learning process for short-term pleasure. Education gives us new information and adds immensely to what we do with our lives. Education often requires giving up something in the present to gain future knowledge or skills to last the rest of our lives. If you don't have much time to read, there are some wonderful, motivational cassettes.

Vocational

How well are we doing our daily jobs? It's been said that a sign of maturity is to be productive and share the fruits of that productivity. Certainly productivity includes the services offered by professionals and business persons as well as the love, grace, and work of those who have chosen raising children as their primary responsibility. As service providers, the better professionals we are, the more opportunities available to use in our working lives. These opportunities provide new directions for our lives. Good professionalism may also spawn relationships offering financial opportunities. However, our concentration should be on giving to our world all we can as its servants, and hopefully the rest follows. Even when it does not, we have the satisfaction of knowing we are doing our best.

Spiritual

Do our lives glorify God? Have we found a way to transform the ordinary tasks of life into something sacred? Although our belief in God may be based on a specific religion with all its dogma, God's commitment to us is unconditional. We only need to be open to life's blessings to receive His love. Nothing can compare with God's love in helping us deal with life's greatest moments. We need His presence to enable us to fully immerse our lives in a world He has created. When our worldly powers fail, God's powers, which are not of this world, are with us.

Financial

To what extent have we established goals for ourselves that cut across the eight pathways? Are we satisfied with our level of savings or do we need to make savings more of a priority in our lives? Living a life style within our means is a must for controlling our lives and making an investment in our future. And when we invest we need to invest on a diversified basis that takes the tax laws into account.

Recreational

What do we do just for fun? Are there times when we have no objective in our actions? For many of us, recreation is a strong point because there are so many entertaining things to do. We can list recreational activities to determine if there's a proper balance among music, movies, reading, television, games, and travel and vacations. For many people, it's almost impossible to take and enjoy a vacation. But this is a very important part of recreational activity requiring long-range planning and follow through. Even though business may be more hectic before and after some time away from the work place, vacations provide time for our spiritual and emotional batteries to recharge and allow us a chance to reflect on where we are directing our lives.

The Balance Wheel

The identification of how our activities fit into the eight major areas of our lives helps us examine whether we are living our lives in balance.

As presented in the previous chapter, visualize in Figure 15.1 concentric circles, labeled between 1 and 10, one for the closest to the center, ten for the farthest out. You can draw a partial circle in the balance wheel for each area of our life based on your internal evaluation. This shows you the extent you are maintaining a balance in your life. Even though you may be doing super in the physical area because you eat well and exercise regularly, give yourself a score of less than 10 initially. There is always some room for improvement.

Once a balance wheel or chart has been made, develop some plans to create more balance in your life. We should work on improving all aspects of our lives but give special attention to the area or areas appearing the most out of balance. Write down action plans to remedy deficiencies and move forward. Even if you don't achieve what you set out to do, you are a winner for making

~·~ WHEEL OF PROGRESS ~·~

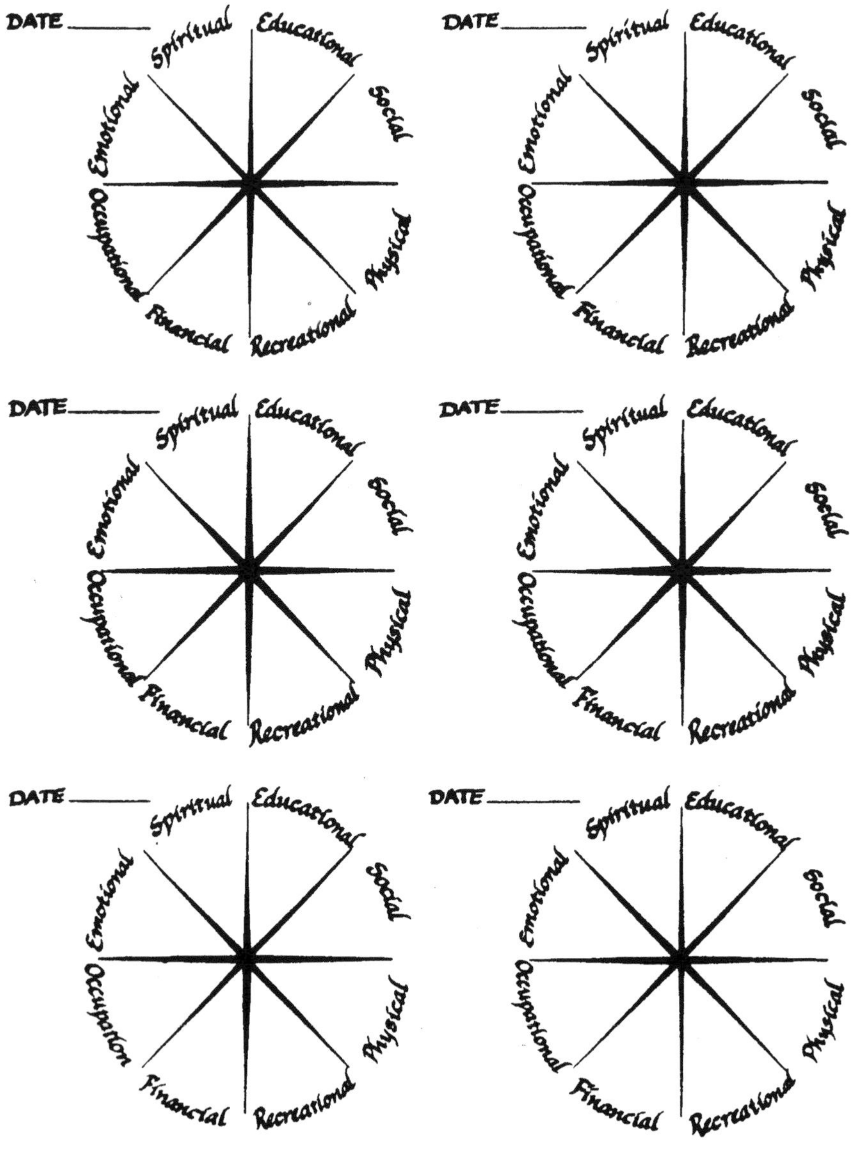

Figure 15.1

the effort.

Establishing a Value System

A challenge we each face is to identify and prioritize our values. We need to know not only what is important in our lives but also how those things that are important compare with each other.

A basic approach is to follow the same process used in the prior chapter. As we identify action steps, we can characterize the action steps as falling in one or more of the eight categories listed in the prior section.

For illustrative purposes, let's take a look at the beginnings of a value system for an individual:

WHAT IS MOST IMPORTANT? Family.

WHY? It is the source of our deepest feelings and most enduring commitments. The growth and development of each family member is challenging, complex and a rewarding task.

WHAT DO WE NEED TO DO? Do fun things together (recreational and social). Pray together at mealtime (spiritual). Learn about new things together and go to new places together (educational). Do special things with spouse including enjoying a robust sex life (physical, recreational, and emotional). Give lots of love to family members (social). Plan a family budget (financial).

WHAT IS THE SECOND MOST IMPORTANT? Profession.

WHY? It is what we have to offer the world. Our work is a benefit we bestow on others in exchange for financial reward which allows us to pay our way in life. It is through our work that we serve others.

WHAT DO WE NEED TO DO? Keep current on changes in our profession (educational). Develop relationships with other professionals so that there can be a networking of interest and opportunities (social and vocational). Strive for professional perfection (vocational). Respond to clients, patients or business peers in a timely, compassionate manner (social and vocational). Manage the cash flow of our business (financial).

WHAT IS THIRD MOST IMPORTANT? Religion.

WHY? Our religion provides us with a source of strength during the tough times in our life. It helps us answer the questions of what is life all about, how we live life to the fullest, and what happens to us when we die.

WHAT DO WE NEED TO DO? Thank the Lord frequently for the wonderful playland he has created for us with all kinds of neat people and fantastic opportunities (spiritual). Attend our place of worship regularly (spiritual). Develop outreach groups and be charitable to others (social and emotional).

WHAT IS FOURTH MOST IMPORTANT? Friendships.

WHY? It is by loving others that we develop our own internal self-love. By sowing the seeds of love and understanding with others, we can reap the rewards of love and understanding within ourselves. Also, sharing experiences and concerns with many different types of people can add new dimensions to our life.

WHAT DO WE NEED TO DO? Invite friends (and if appropriate, their children) to our house for an afternoon (social and recreational). Go to plays, the symphony, movies, sporting events, with friends (social, recreational, emotional and educational). Find out enough about what our friends are doing in their business so that they can be a source of networking (educational, vocational).

And we could go on. If you write down your values and develop action steps for how to get to where you want to go, you can more easily maintain a productive, healthy balance in your life.

The Growth Process

Growth is a continuous process. Growth is moving from fear towards confidence, from compulsion towards choice, and from isolation to intimacy. Fear is a feeling from which follow the actions compulsion and isolation. Confidence is a feeling from which follow the actions choice and intimacy. Feelings and actions can be very closely related. For most of us, it is easier to control our actions than it is to control our feelings. But we need goals in order to establish action plans. Once we know where we choose to go, we can develop some confidence in our ability to get there. If we don't have goals, we may find other people will start making decisions for us - and then we're headed where they want us to go.

If ever in doubt about what to do, let love be your guide. As has been said,

"Only one life to live that soon is past, only what's done with love will last." Source Unknown.

Becoming a Life master

Completing this book should be viewed as the beginning of becoming a life master of the financial game — not the end. The principles and ideas presented herein need to be applied on a constant basis to achieve your own personal level of financial success.

In short, these pages need to be used, not just read. Refer to this book frequently to monitor the plans you have put into action and to challenge the goals you have made for your future financial success.

APPENDIX A
ASSET PROTECTION

By: Robert W. Buechner

If your business or profession exposes you to the potential of litigation, a primary concern should be asset protection.

One of the keys to an effective program of asset protection is the reason given for the steps taken: Any transfer of property to avoid the claims of creditors could be deemed by the courts to be a fraudulent conveyance voidable upon court order. On the other hand, transfers for estate planning purposes, income tax reasons, investment convenience, etc., should be accepted by the courts as valid transfers.

Following are some suggestions on how to protect your assets. The reasoning behind these ideas, their implementation and the protection they offer are discussed.

1. **Spousal Transfers**

With spousal transfers, assets are taken out of joint name and divided between husband and wife, or the spouse with the exposure transfers significant assets into the other spouse's name. Each spouse with assets in his or her name may then transfer the assets to a revocable inter vivos (between living persons) trust.

Estate planning considerations often mandate that each spouse have separate assets in his or her name in order to fully utilize an inter vivos trust. This is a common step in the estate planning process to avoid probate.

The liability or malpractice of one spouse should not put the assets owned solely by the other spouse at risk. While the funding of the inter vivos trust does not protect assets from creditors, it can help reduce probate costs.

2. **Formation of Equipment Corporation**

A physician's spouse and children establish an S corporation to purchase equipment and lease it to the physician's professional corporation. The children are given non-voting common stock so they will not have any say in the management of the equipment corporation.

Income tax considerations can be the reason parents transfer property into the names of children. Children under the age of 14 can receive up to $1,200 of income that is taxed on a favorable basis and children 14 and over have their own income tax brackets. The ownership of S corporation stock can produce taxable income that is taxed at lower tax brackets. It would not be possible for the spouse or children to own any shares of the professional corporation because only a professional can own shares of a professional corporation.

If the physician and his corporation are successfully sued for malpractice, the professional corporation may have to cough up all its assets if the recovery exceeds the malpractice insurance policy limitations. However, the assets of the equipment corporation would not be at risk in the lawsuit since they would be owned independently of the professional corporation. The owner of equipment, unless because of some type of equipment malfunction, could not legitimately be made a party to a malpractice lawsuit. Thus, the physician would still have available to him the equipment he needs for his professional practice.

3. **Transfer Property to Children**

Gifts are made periodically to children (if children are minors, under the uniform gifts to minors act). The gifts can be cash or appreciated property. Significant assets are built up in the children's names for payment of college expenses or the downpayment on the purchase of a home.

For the reasons discussed above, valid income tax reasons exist for getting assets into children's names.

The assets of children should not be exposed to liability in the event a judgment is rendered against a parent.

4. **Build-up of Assets in Qualified Plans**

Qualified plans are an excellent aid for substantial wealth accumulation. Deductible contributions and tax deferred compound growth are twin combatants of the ravages of income taxes and inflation. Upon the termination of the plan or upon termination of employment, the distributed assets can be rolled over tax-free to an IRA.

Practically everyone should be a participant in a qualified plan or IRA to provide for retirement. Social Security is not immune from government cuts and each of us should plan for his own financial independence at retirement rather than be dependent on the federal government.

Qualified plan assets are given special protection by federal law (which generally preempt state law in this area) from the claims of creditors. In addition, certain states like Florida have very solid statutes protecting IRA accounts. Be certain to check your state's laws for IRA protection.

5. **Purchase of Home, Annuities, and High Cash Value Life Insurance**

Everyone needs a place to live and the federal government, through tax incentives, encourages home ownership so it stands to reason everyone should own a home. Annuities and high cash value life insurance are part of valid planning for retirement and may be purchased for sound business and economic reasons.

Now, the good news is that certain states, again like Florida, exempt a home, annuities, and the cash value of life insurance contracts from the claims of creditors in a bankruptcy proceeding. If you're beginning to think it is very important to be able to choose your forum for waging your asset protection battles, you're absolutely right. It is also very helpful to have the right assets in place prior to having to face a possible bankruptcy.

6. **Formation of Family Limited Partnership**

A family limited partnership can only be formed by strict compliance with the applicable state law regarding limited partnerships. There must be a general partner (usually a corporation) and one or more limited partners. A certificate has to be filed at the state and county level disclosing information about the partnership. Usually the parents and children will each be a limited partner to the extent of their contribution to the partnership. The general partner should not be controlled by either parent.

Because all of the assets of a family limited partnership are held as a unit, investment convenience and efficiency are achieved. In addition, previous gifts made to minor children that are contributed to the partnership can be controlled past attainment of age 18 by exercising control of distribution from the family limited partnership. This can be very important to generous parents who are concerned about their children's level of responsibility at age 18.

Anyone who obtains a judgment against an individual who is a limited partner can get a charging order against the partnership. This means the creditor becomes an assignee of the limited partner's interest. As such it appears the creditor stands in the same position as the limited partner in terms of being taxed on a pro rata share of partnership income as well as being able to receive any distribution that would be made to the partner. However, unless the creditor can somehow get control of the general partner (which should be prevented by not allowing someone likely to be exposed to liability to control the corporate general partner), the creditor can not force distribution from the partnership. Thus, the creditor may stand in the position of being taxed on income that is never distributed. Meanwhile, the general partner can pay management fees, etc. to the non-encumbered spouse to keep the family's cash flow going. Thus, a family limited partnership can be an excellent vehicle of asset protection.

7. **Irrevocable Trust**

An irrevocable trust can be established for your spouse and children and funded on a current basis. The trust can be used to purchase life insurance or it can be used to pay out current benefits to the spouse and children. Typically such a trust would contain a spendthrift provision so that a creditor could not reach the trust assets.

An irrevocable trust can be an excellent vehicle of estate planning. If life insurance is purchased, the life insurance can be kept out of both the husband's and wife's estates. If life insurance is not purchased, substantial assets can still be transferred to the trust on an estate tax free basis. But the trust should not utilize the unlimited marital deduction if it is designed to provide current income to the spouse to make certain it does not get caught by the Internal Revenue Code Section 2036(c) snag.

Once the husband has made the gift to the irrevocable trust for solid estate planning reasons, the gift cannot be reached by the husband's creditors. Also, creditors of the spouse and children would have difficulty reaching trust assets because of the spendthrift provisions.

8. **Foreign Situs Trust**

Assets can be transferred from any irrevocable trust to a trust in a foreign jurisdiction that does not give full force and credit to judgments in the United States. Thus a creditor would have to refile in a foreign territory to stake a claim to his rightful share of trust assets. This mechanism simply adds another layer on top of the foregoing methods of asset protection

9. **Other Considerations**

Some experts on asset protection are charging as much as $15,000 (plus a yearly fee) for the formation of a family limited partnership with a foreign situs trust alternative. Other approaches are significantly less expensive. Whatever the expense, it must be measured against the cost of alternatives such as increasing malpractice coverage, purchasing umbrella coverage, or being prepared to move to a state like Florida with favorable bankruptcy laws.

No asset protection program is failsafe. Clients need to be encouraged to take tax and investment planning steps that are consistent with asset protection concerns. The blending of asset protection approaches with other financial concerns can have great benefits.

APPENDIX B
A SOCIAL SECURITY ALTERNATIVE

By: Robert W. Buechner
Guest Columnist for the *Cincinnati Enquirer*
February 25, 1983

Established originally as a supplemental retirement program, Social Security has since developed into a massive welfare system for both the rich and the poor. Its drain on our nation's resources increases each year. Constant funding problems stem from the ill-conceived pay as you go approach that fails to build necessary reserves for the future. Financially insolvent, Social Security is also philosophically bankrupt.

As a retirement program, Social Security is a fraud because it does not base benefits on contributions. As a welfare system, it misses the mark because it does not base benefits on needs. Finally, Social Security discourages savings at a time when savings are crucial to our economy.

Let's admit Social Security is a disaster and talk about a new system.

To begin, eliminate Social Security completely for everyone under 40. Over one-half of the work population is age 35 or younger and this segment of our population does not want Social Security as a noose around its neck. For these people a mandatory savings system should be established which will require a contribution of after-tax dollars of seven percent of each employee's pay, matched by the employer.

These mandatory savings accounts would be completely portable and would provide for no distributions prior to retirement except for death or a permanent disability. In other words, this mandatory savings system would force people to save for the future and to provide for their own retirement. The amount of savings would approximate what is presently being contributed to Social Security except that there would be no lid on one's income subject to the seven percent contribution obligation.

For people 40 and over, make Social Security optional. The ones who want to continue in the system can continue and the ones who want out would be covered by the same mandatory savings system as for people under age 40. Each person then would decide what would be more advantageous economically. There could even be some refund to those who elect out on the basis of the Social Security benefit earned to date and the number of years to retirement.

For the present retirees and for those who elect to continue to be covered by Social Security, funding becomes an enormous problem. Since the Age Discrimination Act now recognizes age 70 as the minimum age at which an employee can be forced to retire, Social Security is out of sync. Why should the elderly of this country be encouraged to terminate employment at age 65 when their talent and experience are so desperately needed? Moreover,
there is no reason why our country should treat vital and vibrant individuals as a liability at the youthful age of 65. The life expectancy for the 65-year-old male has increased dramatically in the past 15 years. Our concept of age has been changing for purposes of exercise, sex, longevity, productivity - for everything except Social Security.

We should increase the age at which a worker can be eligible for full Social Security benefits to 70, although we must do this gradually to avoid unfairness to those who have counted on retiring at 65 and are near that age.

But increasing the retirement age only helps with part of the funding crisis. What should be done about the massive funding obligation that remains? The mandatory savings accounts could be used as a source of cash for Social Security with the government paying Treasury Bill rates on the money borrowed to fund Social Security. In this way there would be no immediate net cash drain on the federal government (or on the country's cash reserves), although clearly over a period of time someone would have to pay for the borrowings from the mandatory savings accounts. At least, the liability for the Social Security program would have an ending date.

Suppose the mandatory savings program does not provide enough money for an individual's retirement, what then? In this situation, assuming there are no other sources of funds, the retired individual could apply for a senior assistance check. Senior assistance would work the same as any other type of welfare and would be based on demonstrated need. This type of program would serve a definite but limited purpose and would not pretend to be all things to all people.

The mandatory savings plan outlined here would base retirement benefits on contributions and senior assistance benefits on need. It would encourage older employees to work longer. It would eliminate gradually the Social Security drain; and it would increase savings. Don't you agree this approach makes more sense?

APPENDIX C

Single Life, unisex, 10 percent showing the present worth of an annuity, of a life interest, and of a remainder interest

1 Age	2 Annuity	3 Life Estate	4 Remainder
0	9.7188	97188	02812
1	9.8988	.98988	.01012
2	9.9017	.99017	.00983
3	9.9008	.99008	.00992
4	9.8981	.98981	.01019
5	9.8938	.98938	.01062
6	9.8884	.98884	.01116
7	9.8822	.98822	.01178
8	9.8748	.98748	.01252
9	9.8663	.98663	.01337
10	9.8565	.98565	.01435
11	9.8453	.98453	.01547
12	9.8329	.98329	.01671
13	9.8198	.98198	.01802
14	9.8066	.98066	.01934
15	9.7937	.97937	.02063
16	9.7815	.97815	.02185
17	9.7700	.97700	.02300
18	9.7590	.97590	.02410
19	9.7480	.97480	.02520
20	9.7365	.97365	.02635
21	9.7245	.97245	.02755
22	9.7120	.97120	.02880
23	9.6986	.96986	.03014
24	9.6841	.96841	.03159
25	9.6678	.96678	.03322
26	9.6495	.96495	.03505
27	9.6290	.96290	.03710
28	9.6062	.96062	.03938
29	9.5813	.95813	.04187

1 Age	2 Annuity	3 Life Estate	4 Remainder
55	8.0046	.80046	.19954
56	7.9006	.79006	.20994
57	7.7931	.77931	.22069
58	7.6822	.76822	.23178
59	7.5675	.75675	.24325
60	7.4491	.74491	.25509
61	7.3267	.73267	.26733
62	7.2002	.72002	.27998
63	7.0696	.70696	.29304
64	6.9352	.69352	.30648
65	6.7970	.67970	.32030
66	6.6551	.66551	.33449
67	6.5098	.65098	.34902
68	6.3610	.63610	.36390
69	6.2086	.62086	.37914
70	6.0522	.60522	.39478
71	5.8914	.58914	.41086
72	5.7261	.57261	.42739
73	5.5571	55571	.44429
74	5.3862	.53862	.46138
75	5.2149	.52149	.47851
76	5.0441	.50441	.49559
77	4.8742	.48742	.51258
78	4.7049	.47049	.52951
79	4.5357	.45357	.54643
80	4.3659	.43659	.56341
81	4.1967	.41967	.58033
82	4.0295	.40295	.59705
83	3.8642	.38642	.61358
84	3.6998	.36998	.63002

1 Age	2 Annuity	3 Life Estate	4 Remainder
30	9.5543	.95543	.04457
31	9.5254	.95254	.04746
32	9.4942	.94942	.05058
33	9.4608	.94608	.05392
34	9.4250	.94250	.05750
35	9.3868	.93868	.06132
36	9.3460	.93460	.06540
37	9.3026	.93026	.06974
38	9.2567	.92567	.07433
39	9.2083	.92083	.07917
40	9.1571	.91571	.08429
41	9.1030	.91030	.08970
42	9.0457	.90457	.09543
43	8.9855	.89855	.10145
44	8.9221	.89221	.10779
45	8.8558	.88558	.11442
46	8.7863	.87863	.12137
47	8.7137	.87137	.12863
48	8.6374	.86374	.13626
49	8.5578	.85578	.14422
50	8.4743	.84743	.15257
51	8.3874	.83874	.16126
52	8.2969	.82969	.17031
53	8.2028	.82028	.17972
54	8.1054	.81054	.18946

1 Age	2 Annuity	3 Life Estate	4 Remainder
85	3.5359	.35359	.64641
86	3.3764	.33764	.66236
87	3.2262	.32262	.67738
88	3.0859	.30859	.69141
89	2.9526	.29526	.70474
90	2.8221	.28221	.71779
91	2.6955	.26955	.73045
92	2.5771	.25771	.74229
93	2.4692	.24692	.75308
94	2.3728	.23728	.76272
95	2.2887	.22887	.77113
96	2.2181	.22181	.77819
97	2.1550	.21550	.78450
98	2.1000	.21000	.79000
99	2.0486	.20486	.79514
100	1.9975	.19975	.80025
101	1.9532	.19532	.80468
102	1.9054	.19054	.80946
103	1.8437	.18437	.81563
104	1.7856	.17856	.82144
105	1.6962	.16962	.83038
106	1.5488	.15488	.84512
107	1.3409	.13409	.86591
108	1.0068	.10068	.89932
109	.4545	.04545	.95455

Treasury Regulation Sections 20.2031-10 and 252512-9

INDEX